One at the Table
The Reception of Baptized Christians

# Font and Table Series

The Font and Table Series offers pastoral perspectives on Christian baptism, confirmation and eucharist.

One at the Table
The Reception of Baptized Christians

RONALD A. OAKHAM, O. CARM.

KATHY BROWN

RITA FERRONE

JOSEPH FAVAZZA

MARK SEARLE

Liturgy Training Publications

ACKNOWLEDGMENTS

Excerpts from United States edition of the *Rite of Christian Initiation of Adults* (Chicago: Liturgy Training Publications, 1988), © 1985, International Committee on English in the Liturgy, © 1988, United States Catholic Conference. All rights reserved. Excerpts from the Canadian edition are © 1985, International Committee on English in the Liturgy; © 1985, Canadian Catholic Conference. All rights reserved. Excerpts from National Statutes for the Catechumenate, © 1988, United States Catholic Conference. All rights reserved.

Chapter 4, "The Effects of Baptism," by Mark Searle, first appeared in the July 1990 issue (vol. 12, no. 4) of *Catechumenate: A Journal of Christian Initiation.*

Acquisitions editor: Victoria M. Tufano
Production editor: Deborah E. Bogaert
Designer: Barb Rohm
Production artist: Jim Mellody-Pizzato
This book was typeset in Centaur and Frutiger and printed by Commercial Communications, Inc.

Library of Congress Cataloging-in-Publications Data
Oakham, Ronald A.
    One at the table : the reception of baptized Christians / Ronald A.
Oakham ... [et al.].
        p. cm. — (Font and table series)
    Includes bibliographical references (p. 159).
    1. Catholic Church — United States — Reception of baptized Christians.
    2. Catholic Church — United States — Membership. 3. Catholic Church —
United States — Liturgy. 4. Pastoral theology — Catholic Church. I. Title.
    II. Series.
    BX2045.R38025 1995   95-26408
    264'.02099 — DC20   CIP
ISBN 1-56854-070-1
ONETBL

CONTENTS

INTRODUCTION

I believe it is true to say that practicing Roman Catholics who were at least eight years old in 1964 carry definite memories of the implementation of the new Roman Missal and how it effected monumental changes in the church's way of celebrating the eucharist. The same cannot be said, however, of their memories about the promulgation of the provisional English translation of the *Rite of Christian Initiation of Adults* in 1974. This text entered the life of the church in North America without any of the fanfare that accompanied many of the other revised sacraments. In some circles it was deemed to have been designed for "mission territories," which characterized neither the United States nor Canada, and so it was discreetly placed on library shelves to gather dust. Implementation became the prerogative of individual parishes spurred on by visionaries of evangelization on the parish staff and/or within the community.

Pastoral interest in the rite was generated in part through the work of Christiane Brusselmans (a theologian and catechist from Belgium), who, from 1978 to 1981, gathered pastoral ministers, sacramental theologians and liturgists in various locations for symposia, workshops and conferences to explore and promote the restoration of the catechumenate. Upon the foundations she and her colleagues laid, the North American Forum on the Catechumenate was built in October 1981. Among the strategies that Forum used to promote the catechumenate was the identification and further training of people already engaged in the pastoral work of the order of initiation. These people then served as team members for institutes sponsored by Forum and by dioceses and institutions throughout North America and beyond. Forum's efforts to foster the implementation of the adult initiation rites were given further impetus when revised English editions of the *Rite of Christian Initiation of Adults* were put into effect by the national conferences of Catholic bishops in Canada (1987) and the United States (1988).

Through the initial years of implementation, much of the attention given to the order of Christian initiation focused on the initiation of unbaptized adults (as outlined in part I of the ritual text). This was most appropriate because this renewed order sought to reform not only the sacramental rites but also our whole perception of initiation and church membership as well. Therefore, we needed to (and, indeed, still need to) dwell in this new world, plumbing its depths and searching its horizons for renewed understandings of Christian initiation.

Through all these years of "discovery," pastoral practitioners in both the United States and Canada have been involved more in the reception of adults already baptized in other Christian communities than in the initiation of unbaptized adults. Thus they continually ask about adaptations of the order for baptized Christians seeking to enter into the full communion of the Catholic church. Unfortunately, they often are concerned with the adaptation of the rites of initiation before they understand the basic design and underlying theology of these rites. Forum's team members have challenged their colleagues in ministry to strive to understand the foundational vision presented in part I of the ritual text first, and then to move on to making adaptations. Without this understanding, any adaptation risks being both pastorally and theologically unsound.

Over the past few years, I have become concerned that, with our growing appreciation of both the marvels effected in people's lives through catechumenal formation and the power of initiatory rites well celebrated, we also may be eroding our theology of baptism. Because little attention has been given to the initiation of baptized Christians (except for some ritual aspects), many initiation ministers are treating baptized Christians in much the same way they treat unbaptized persons. I believe this is happening because the primary focus, spurred on by our educationally oriented church, has been on the level of catechetical formation, particularly doctrinal instruction. While it is true that a baptized Christian's formation often is as lacking as an unbaptized person's, a different spiritual reality exists in the life of the baptized person, catechized or not. To rest sacramental efficacy on catechetical formation and personal responsiveness is to jeopardize our theology of baptism.

Out of this concern, while I was a member of the Forum staff, I began to address the question of adaptations for baptized Christians in various articles I wrote for *Catechumenate: A Journal of Christian Initiation.* These articles (which are listed in the bibliography at the end of this book) led me into some interesting conversations with my Forum colleagues, some of whom agree and some of whom disagree with my perspective. Both sides of the discussion have engendered in me a desire to pursue the questions. This book is my latest attempt at grappling with this complex issue. To this end, I am approaching the topic with a two-fold focus that is reflected in the organization of this book: The chapters in part I focus on theological issues, and the chapters in part II focus on pastoral implementation.

Kathy Brown, a pastoral theologian who was a colleague of mine on Forum's staff for a period of time and has become a good friend, is the author of the first chapter. It shares her experience of coming to grips with the issue at hand in her pastoral setting. Kathy's contribution here is like the overture of a musical, in which we hear parts of the various themes to be developed in the full performance of the work. Kathy's chapter includes both theological and pastoral explorations.

Chapters two through five have been written to stimulate your theological consciousness. In chapter two Rita Ferrone, a liturgical theologian who has a delightful knack for viewing things from a slightly different perspective, surveys the underlying theology of reception into the full communion of the Catholic Church. Joseph Favazza, a sacramental theologian who has contributed to my own deeper understanding of the sacrament of penance, sheds light on the reconciliation question in chapter three. Chapter four is an article by the late Mark Searle originally written for *Catechumenate: A Journal of Christian Initiation* (vol. 12, no. 4; July, 1990). Though I never knew Mark personally, we were, in a sense, collaborators in delving into the question of adaptations for the baptized Christian. It began with a discussion with Jim Wilde, then the editor of *Catechumenate*, regarding possible articles for the magazine. I told Jim that I wanted to explore the question of Lenten rites and the baptized Christian, but I felt I needed a foundation to build upon, namely, an article on baptism. This article by Mark Searle is what Jim arranged. I have written the final chapter of part I, which identifies my understanding of what the renewed order of Christian initiation is setting forth as the normative dimensions for all initiation.

I am the sole author of part II, but the material in these chapters is not solely my own. These chapters include stories of pastoral work that I gathered through a case study. Using Forum's network of pastoral ministers, I contacted 67 parish catechumenate coordinators throughout the United States and Canada, searching for those who are striving to be sensitive in a concrete manner to the differences between the unbaptized and the baptized. I received responses from 22 coordinators. Ten of them indicated that they were not attending to this issue with more than the ritual sensitivity already included in the ritual text. From the 12 parishes that are responding to the situation more intentionally, I have included stories from the ten that I was able to interview. (I am sure there are other parishes doing good pastoral adaptations. Their absence in this case study is not based on a judgment of their efforts but is due to the limits of time.)

Following these pastoral responses, I include in each chapter my ruminations about the issues that these parishes are dealing with, in light of the theological points from part I and these pastoral practices. My intention in this section of the book is to share models that are being developed by good pastoral practitioners. I also share my thoughts about these issues to prompt readers' own critical thinking and, I hope, to further the development of the initiation process within their own pastoral situations.

ACKNOWLEDGMENTS

This book would not have been possible without the responsiveness of a number of initiation ministers in the field. I am thankful for the work done by the other authors, to the 22 catechumenate coordinators who responded to my inquiry, and in particular to those whose stories I have used: Marydith Chase, St. Philip the Apostle in Bakersfield, California; Jerry Galipeau and Mary Fontana, St. Marcelline in Schaumburg, Illinois; John Butler, St. Augustine in Washington, D.C.; Marguerite Main, St. Louise in Bellevue, Washington; Chuck Barthel, Mary, Mother of the Church in St. Louis, Missouri; Nick Wagner and Peggy Lovrien, Most Holy Trinity in San Jose, California; Diane Banks and Paul Turner, St. John Francis Regis in Kansas City, Missouri; Todd Flowerday, St. Margaret Mary in Algonquin, Illinois; Theresa Frey, St. Vincent de Paul in Weyburn, Saskatchewan; and Tim Ziegler, Holy Cross in Regina, Saskatchewan.

THINGS TO NOTE WHILE READING THIS BOOK

PARAGRAPH REFERENCES

When reference is made to resource material, the book or article will be cited in an endnote. For references to material from the *Rite of Christian Initiation of Adults,* however, the paragraph numbers will be given in parentheses. When the paragraph numbers for the U.S. and Canadian editions differ, both will be given. The National Statutes are found in appendix III of the U.S. edition.

REFERENCES TO THE RITE OF RECEPTION INTO THE FULL COMMUNION OF THE CATHOLIC CHURCH

Because the title of this rite is long and (as you will read in Rita Ferrone's article) theologically exact, it is difficult to use a shortened name. But for the sake of efficiency, throughout this book the terms "Rite of Reception" or "reception into the church" will be used. Please note that each author does so with the full understanding of the exactness of the full title.

DEDICATION

This book is dedicated to all my Forum colleagues with whom I have worked over the years, to the other staff members at the central office in northern Virginia and to the numerous team members on institutes, but especially to Jim Dunning, the founder of Forum, who died in September of 1995 as this book was being prepared for publication. The commitment of all of these people to critical study and reflection about initiation and to pastoral integrity in implementation, along with their excitement and delight in the experience of accompanying others on the journey to the Lord's table, have been a source of inspiration and formation for me. Much of what I have written is the weaving of ideas and understandings to which they have contributed. I am deeply indebted to them.

PART I

Theological Foundations

CHAPTER 1

Expanding the Limits of Initiation

KATHY BROWN

Marty, Melanie, Steve and David are real people (names changed) who asked to become Catholic. Because their stories challenged our parish's initiation principles, the parish catechumenate team and pastoral staff had to reexamine what it means to be a Catholic Christian, how we initiate, and what our expectations are of someone who is becoming a Catholic.

It was the early 1980s, and I was attempting to implement for the first time the *Rite of Christian Initiation of Adults.* The general practice at that time was to put everyone who wanted to become Catholic into the same six- to nine-month program. Little distinction was made, either in liturgical celebrations or in the preparation process, between a person who was baptized and a person who was not baptized, or between somenone who was catechized and someone who was not catechized. Even the language of the rites referred to all the candidates for initiation as "catechumens."

During these initial years of implementation, one of the first issues our parish staff struggled with was whether or not to include Catholics returning to the church in the same sessions as those preparing to become Catholic. Our experience led us to conclude that returning Catholics needed special sessions designed for their specific needs. This was the beginning of my experience with differentiation in the initiation process.

By the mid to late 1980s, it became evident to me and to many other initiation ministers throughout the United States and Canada that not all the men and women seeking to explore the Catholic tradition were beginning at the same point. Many of those who came to us were already evangelized. In other words, their lives had brought them into contact with the Christian life in many ways, and they already were living many dimensions of the gospel. Even being unbaptized did not necessarily mean that a person was not evangelized or was totally uncatechized. Consequently, during those years we focused on clearly distinguishing between catechumens and candidates, especially in the language of the rites, and on acknowledging the level of faith with which they came to us.

Now, in the first half of the 1990s, our parish initiation team has been focusing on the issue of who belongs in an extended initiation process (the full catechumenate) and who needs a less intensive process. For us this question has prompted deeper reflection on initiation theology and on the pastoral ramifications for those who come seeking to join us.

As I travel throughout the United States and Canada, it is clear to me that there is confusion and, in some cases, a growing resentment toward and resistance to using the catechumenate in its fullest form. Parish personnel in particular struggle with the order of initiation not because of the rites themselves but because of what they see as unnecessary conditions put upon people who may not need an extended process for initiation. In other words, we have begun to recognize that not all people seeking to become Catholic are unevangelized or uncatechized.

At present, however, parish initiation processes are tending at best to perfect the process in place or at worst to fossilize what they are offering as the parish's one initiation program. As Ron Oakham unfortunately found in his interviews with parishes throughout the United States and Canada, in both the best and worst scenarios little is being done to provide suitable alternatives for those who do not require a full catechumenate experience for initiation. Even less is being done to develop a process for determining who should and should not participate in the full catechumenate process. Consequently, a struggle has emerged for some pastoral ministers. They either continue to resist implementing the revised order of Christian initiation or want to "downsize," if not eliminate, the initiation process (at least in its current form of implementation).

The reality is that the *Rite of Christian Initiation of Adults* is the Roman way of initiating at this time in our history. If it is to be implemented appropriately, however, the concern raised about who belongs in an extended initiation process needs to be addressed.

This article raises the question of how we respond to people who come to us asking to become Catholic and who do not fit into either the catechumenate or an adapted process for baptized, uncatechized Christians. A corollary concern is how a parish initiation team discerns who belongs in the catechumenate, with its periods and rites, and who needs a separate process of preparation for reception into the church. Are there some criteria by which we can judge (*Rite of Christian Initiation of Adults*, #119 U.S., 106 Can.; unless otherwise noted, all references are to this document) a person's readiness for reception? If there is a separate track for those who are baptized and do not belong in the parish's catechumenate, then how does a parish welcome and prepare them for reception and provide continued care for them after reception?

WHO BELONGS IN THE CATECHUMENATE?

The restored catechumenate is intended primarily for unbaptized adults and children of catechetical age. The language used in the order (e.g., "catechumen, elect") pertains mostly to those preparing to become Christian. Because the *Rite of Christian Initiation of Adults* is the norm for initiation for the entire church, it includes provisions for adaptations that allow parishes to minister to those who come to us baptized—yet uncatechized—and desiring to become Catholic. In fact, the majority of those seeking to become Catholic in the United States and Canada are baptized in other Christian denominations.

Those who are baptized but uncatechized ("candidates," as we have come to call them, short for "candidates for reception into full communion") are often on a journey of faith parallel to that of catechumens. The ritual text provides adapted rites that respect the baptism of these candidates, anticipating that their pastoral formation also will parallel that of the catechumens. Thus, in most parishes it is common practice for the catechumens and candidates to come together for their initiation sessions and celebrations. But making use of the adapted rites while catechizing the candidates and catechumens together, without providing appropriate adjustments, is not enough. (This topic will be addressed more fully later in this book.)

There is yet a third group of people who come to us asking to become Catholic. These are adults who are baptized and generally catechized (formally or informally) and who may be ready to be received into the full communion of the Catholic church rather than participating in the extensive pastoral formation provided in a catechumenal process. It is with this group that the most recent questions arose in our parish as to what is suitable for their initiation.

In the excitement that accompanies the implementation of the order of initiation, many parishes deliver all the people who are interested in becoming Catholic to the doors of the parish's catechumenate. Baptized and unbaptized, catechized and uncatechized together join in sessions meant to draw people into the life of Jesus Christ and his church. But not everyone belongs in the catechumenate, in an extended time of pastoral formation.

Throughout North America, many voices have expressed concern that inquirers, regardless of their religious history or background, are being required to "jump through hoops" in order to become Catholic. People who have been attending Sunday eucharist with their spouses for years are not considered catechized, even though an informal catechesis transpires through the proclamation of the word and through their association with other Catholic Christians. The community activities and service of people who are already deeply committed to living Christian values are not considered in the discernment of their readiness for reception into the church. It is often assumed that the best way to serve all inquirers is to send them through a nine-month or year-long preparation before their automatic reception at the Easter Vigil.

Pastoral experience, however, teaches — and the ritual text presumes — that not all people ought to go through all the periods and rites in the order of Christian initiation. The question is, how does the parish team decide, with the inquirer, the best and most appropriate journey of preparation for reception into the full communion of the Catholic church?

It is essential for a parish initiation team and/or staff to develop the ability to discern where a person is on the journey of faith and how best to serve that person. Out of this discernment is created a method or a process to prepare the inquirer for reception into the Catholic church. To require all people to join the parish's catechumenate even though it may not be appropriate gives the message that we do not accept or respect how God has already been actively involved in the inquirer's life and that we do not truly respect the efficacy of their baptism.

WHAT DOES THE RITE SAY?

In the *Rite of Christian Initiation of Adults,* the Rite of Reception of Baptized Christians into the Full Communion of the Catholic Church states:

> This is the liturgical rite by which a person born and baptized in a separated ecclesial community is received, according to the Latin rite, into the full communion of the Catholic church. The rite is so arranged that no greater

burden than necessary (see Acts 15:28) is required for the establishment of communion and unity. (#473–504 U.S., 387–417 Can.)

The instructions for the rite do not say why a person would celebrate this particular rite rather than participate in the extended pastoral formation intended for catechumens or baptized, uncatechized adults. From a comparison of the instructions for the initiation of unbaptized adults (part I), those for baptized, uncatechized adults (part II, 4) and those for baptized, catechized adults who will participate in the singular rite of reception (part II, 5), however, one may deduce that baptized, catechized candidates are somehow different, and therefore "no greater burden than necessary" is to be required of them for reception into the church. The instructions for reception go on to say that:

> The baptized Christian is to receive both doctrinal and spiritual preparation, adapted to individual pastoral requirements. . . . The candidate should learn to deepen an inner adherence to the church. . . . (#477 U.S., 391 Can.)

Interestingly, the rite's instructions (#478, U.S. only) indicate that the candidate "may benefit from the celebration of liturgical rites marking their progress in formation." Therefore, "one or several of the rites included in part II, 4, 'Preparation of Uncatechized Adults for Confirmation and Eucharist,' may be celebrated as they are presented or in similar words" (#478, U.S. only). In either case, the order emphasizes the importance of discernment regarding the appropriate way to serve the candidate for full communion.

In addition, the assumption cannot be made that the candidate for reception is catechized. According to the instruction quoted earlier, catechesis may be exactly what is necessary to prepare a particular person for the rite of reception, although probably not as extensive a catechesis as that required or needed in the pastoral formation of catechumens. We may need to expand the limits that we have regarding what is essential for initiation. The order seems to suggest that what is needed is a deeper awareness of the elements that contribute to authentic conversion and a broader understanding of readiness for reception into the full communion of the Catholic church.

Given that the norm for initiation is embedded in part I of the *Rite of Christian Initiation of Adults,* we turn to it to understand more fully who the rite of reception is intended for and what our responsibilities are to those going through the rite.

LISTENING AND DISCERNMENT

The greatest gift we offer to people who come to us wanting to become Catholic is our ability to listen to them. Listening with both heart and mind, we discover with them the journey of faith they are on and the best way to minister to them. If I as an initiation minister enter an initial interview with an inquirer with the assumption that this person will fit into the parish catechumenate, then I am being unfaithful to my role as minister. No matter how patiently and respectfully I listen, ask questions and enter into conversation, if in the end I have the same response for every person—that they are to proceed through the catechumenate—then it is possible that I have refused to acknowledge how God has already been active in that person's life.

During the initial interview with someone interested in becoming a Catholic Christian, we begin to listen and discern how best to serve the person. The initial interview is not only an opportunity for acquiring information (baptized, unbaptized, married, divorced, annulled, etc.), it is also, and more importantly, the first step in developing a relationship with the inquirer. We participate in the story of the inquirer by listening and thereby discovering the depth and breadth of a person's relationship with God, with the Christian community at large, with the Catholic church in particular, with this person's neighbors and with the world in which he or she lives. These relationships help lead the person into recognizing the signs of God's presence in his or her life. As we listen to the inquirer tell about these relationships, we keep in mind the vision of what the whole process of initiation is really about. In the light of that vision, we can discover how best to journey with the candidate into oneness at the eucharistic table.

ALLOWING THE VISION TO GUIDE

Throughout the process of initiation in a parish, the team continually needs to ask itself why they are doing what they are doing. What is their purpose, and how do they hope to accomplish it? Refocusing on the purpose of the order of Christian initiation may help us understand not only what we are doing and why we are doing it, but also how to listen to the unfolding stories of the initiate so we can shape a path to the Lord's table that is suitable for them.

The order of initiation is made up of liturgical rites that mark and celebrate a person's conversion to the way of Jesus Christ. The conversion journey of an individual takes place not only *in the midst* of the Christian community but also *with* the Christian community as it walks the same way. Together we strive to live the Christian vocation, which is to be a disciple of Jesus Christ. At its core, the initiation process is about becoming a follower of Jesus Christ, learning to live as a Christian in all of one's life. This journey as a disciple of Jesus Christ leads ultimately to union with the triune God.

The *National Catechetical Directory* (NCD) puts it another way: It states that all catechesis ought to lead to maturity of faith.[1] The NCD is clear that catechesis is not information for the sake of information. Rather, if evangelization is the call to conversion to Jesus Christ, catechesis is the continuing and deepening of that conversion to the God of Jesus Christ. This has social ramifications for a person's whole life. The NCD proposes that care for catechesis (instruction), for integration into the Christian community, for development of the life of prayer and worship and for training in service are all essential elements leading toward maturity of faith. The document goes on to state that maturity in faith includes an intimate relationship with God, a depth of commitment involving the whole of life and rooted in a community of faith.

The *Rite of Christian Initiation of Adults* emphasizes these four elements of Christian formation in paragraph 75. First, it states that a person needs a suitable catechesis that is "gradual and complete" and leads "to a profound sense of the mystery of salvation" (#75.1). Second, the catechumen needs to "become familiar with the Christian way of life" and learn to "turn more readily to God in prayer, to bear witness to the faith, in all things to keep their hopes set on Christ, to follow supernatural inspiration in their deeds, and to practice love of neighbor." This progressive transition becomes "manifest by means of its social consequences" (#75.2). Third, the catechumen is introduced into the prayer and worship of the church through participation in celebrations of the word of God at Mass and other appropriate liturgical rites (#75.3). Fourth, catechumens are drawn into the apostolic life of the church by working "actively with others to spread the gospel and build up the church" (#75.4).

These four elements reflect the ancient dimensions of the life of the church: *kerygma* (word or message), *koinonia* (community), *liturgia* (worship) and *diakonia* (service). Paragraph 78 of the order provides a summary of what takes place during the catechumenate period:

> The instruction that the catechumens receive during this period should be of a kind that while presenting Catholic teaching in its entirety also enlightens faith, directs the heart toward God, fosters participation in the liturgy, inspires apostolic activity, and nurtures a life completely in accord with the spirit of Christ.

Therefore, through all that constitutes the process of initiation, the catechumen or candidate somehow is moved toward fulfillment of the objective stated in paragraph 78, which is maturity of faith.

It seems then that we have a picture of the goal of all the pastoral formation during the catechumenate, both for catechumens and for candidates who are traveling a parallel journey of initiation. Each person is to be catechized in the fullest sense of the word, to be in a relationship with Jesus Christ, to be involved in service or apostolic activity, to be part of the community and its life, and to be living out the gospel in all aspects of their lives. The responsibility of the team is to provide an environment whereby the catechumen and candidate can grow in maturity of faith, which is reflected in the behavior and lifestyle indicative of the Christian life.

This same criteria is not only for catechumens and candidates but for all Christians, including possible candidates for reception into full communion. The initial interview becomes the key to discerning where a person is on this journey of faith. Understanding the dimensions of the fullness of living the Christian way of life, especially as put forward in paragraph 75, serves as a guide for determining the best means of serving the candidate for reception into the full communion of the Catholic church. Where is this inquirer in comprehending the mystery of the Christian faith and the command of that faith for all of life? Is this person connected to the community? Does she or he recognize the social ramifications for living the Christian way of life? Has this person developed a discipline of prayer and worship in tune with the rich tradition of our church? Does she or he recognize and respond to the call of the gospel to be a missionary through service and witness? How we answer these questions will give shape to the type of formation and support we offer in preparation, celebration and ongoing attention to the candidate for reception.

EXAMPLES OF EXCEPTIONS

At the beginning of this article I mentioned the names of several people who did not fit into the normal path of initiation. Each of them required special attention and consideration as the initiation team listened to their stories. What they had in common was that God had been actively present in their lives—that their journeys of conversion had been taking place long before they came to the initial interview—and that each would not need to participate in an extensive catechumenal process.

MARTY AND MELANIE

Marty and Melanie had been married for 16 years. After Marty received an annulment of his previous marriage, they had their marriage blessed in the Catholic church. Melanie, a very strong Catholic, had never pushed Marty to become a Catholic. But because he knew her faith was important to her, he always came to Mass with her on Sundays. Melanie worked for a Catholic high school, and both of them were deeply involved in supporting and serving the school through participation in social outreach programs. Marty was very much at home among Catholics, but he never felt worthy enough to ask to become a Catholic. The pain and devastation of his first marriage left him believing that God did not love him. Therefore, he concluded that the church of God would not want him in its midst. After hearing a homily that he believed was addressed to him, Marty decided to take the step and become a Catholic.

At the initial interview it became clear that Marty did not belong in the parish catechumenate. He had been baptized and catechized in a mainline Protestant church, and after fifteen years of attending Mass with his wife and participating in many outreach activities through the high school, Marty was already living a deeply committed life of faith in the midst of the Catholic Christian community. We recognized two areas he needed to work on in preparation for reception into the Catholic church.

Marty joined the catechumenate for the opportunity to meet other people going through initiation and for an opportunity to reflect more deeply on the scriptures in the context of the liturgical year. Melanie joined him, and together they participated with the catechumens and the baptized, uncatechized candidates in exploring the various pastoral ministries of the parish, including visiting the sick and serving the homeless of the area. At the appropriate time, Marty was received into the full communion of the Catholic church during a Sunday morning liturgy. Marty and Melanie continue to prepare and serve meals at a local shelter and dining room for the poor.

STEVE

Steve had been reaching toward the Catholic church all his life, even though he was raised in a mainline evangelical denomination. Baptized as a teenager, he eventually became a minister in his denomination but continued to be attracted to the Catholic church. He sought spiritual direction at a monastery, worked hard in social justice activities and kept abreast of current theology. Finally, upon moving to Phoenix, he came to grips with his long-time desire not only to become a Catholic but to seek to become a priest. Eventually he found his way to our parish. As his story unfolded it became clear that he did not fit into the parish's normal process for initiation. The pastor was asked to interview him, and from this it was recommended that Steve work with a spiritual director in preparation for becoming Catholic.

As a team we reviewed the criteria of paragraph 75 in determining how to serve him. Catechetically, Steve had integrated the theology of our faith deeply into his life over the years. We identified questions for study, especially in regard to the sacrament of penance and some of the moral teachings of the Catholic church. We also worked with a parish-assigned sponsor to draw Steve into a more active role in parish life through meeting and building relationships with parishioners. Steve's recognition of the call to live an apostolic life was evident in his work for justice for homeless people. In final preparation for reception, the initiation team suggested a private retreat for him guided by his spiritual director. At a Sunday liturgy during the Easter Season, Steve was received into the full communion of the Catholic church.

DAVID

Over one summer, the staff and team members surfaced the names of those people we knew in the parish who were not Catholic but who participated actively in the parish. We extended an invitation to them to join the Catholic church. Several came forward, but one in particular represents many of them. David had been attending Mass with his wife for the 20 years of their marriage. He and his whole family were very active in the parish and known by many people. The informal catechesis that had been taking place for 20 years through homilies and association with Catholics prepared him for his life as a Catholic. He understood clearly the call to service in his life, and prayer and worship were already an essential part of his life. The pastor and members of the initiation team met with him to help uncover his story of where and how God had been working in his life. David had a clear idea of what it meant to be a Catholic, but he had never had the opportunity to explore the depth of his faith, to identify who and where God was in his life and to see his life through the eyes of faith.

Because the team and the pastor thought it essential, David's wife eventually became part of these sessions. Together, they looked at their marriage through the eyes of faith. After celebrating the sacrament of penance, David was received into the full communion of the Catholic church on Pentecost Sunday at the Mass he and his family regularly attended. The whole assembly was able to celebrate this important moment for David and his family. A few weeks later David and his wife renewed their marriage vows.

Throughout their experiences with Marty and Melanie, Steve, David and the many others who inquired about the Catholic church, the initiation team grew in their understanding of faith. We discovered that there are many common elements in people's stories, and that as we listened to the inquirers' stories of God's involvement in their lives, we recognized our own stories. But even though there are common moments of awakening in people's lives that can be celebrated publicly, each person's journey is unique. Everyone's personal history, accumulated pain, desires of the heart, families, work situations and so much more form a singular path to faith. God offers redemption to all in a very personalized way, and this offer of salvation is mediated by and through the community that respects God's involvement in a person's life.

SUMMARY OF THE PROCESS

From the parish initiation team's experience and continued work with a variety of people asking to become Catholic, we have articulated the following guidelines.

1) Every interview will begin with the premise that not all people seeking to become Catholic belong in a catechumenate.

2) The initial interview will be a time of listening with the purpose of helping to discern how best to serve this particular person.

3) The team needs to keep the vision of initiation in focus at all times.

4) The elements of a complete catechesis (word, community, prayer and worship, and ministry) form a background for determining how best to serve and support the faith journey of those seeking initiation into our church.

5) If the Rite of Reception into the Full Communion of the Catholic Church is more appropriate than the catechumenate with all its periods and steps, then the time of preparation will be crafted to meet the individual needs of the candidate.

6) Some type of prayer or retreat needs to be planned for the candidate being received into the church.

7) Continued care and attention will be given to the candidate after reception, just as is necessary with neophytes.

In addition, several assumptions guide our parish initiation team, staff and sponsors in determining the readiness of a candidate to be received into the full communion of the Catholic church. It is assumed that the candidate who is ready for reception

1) has become acquainted and enjoys a relationship with members of the parish community;

2) has had an opportunity to explore the catechetical dimensions of his or her faith;

3) lives a life in tune with the prayer and worship of the parish community and the Catholic tradition;

4) recognizes and is involved in fulfilling the apostolic life of ministry and witness.

At the same time, it is assumed that the candidate is not perfect and, along with so many of us, struggles to live the life we profess as disciples of Jesus Christ.

CHALLENGE AND CONCLUSION

The past 20 years of implementing the order of Christian initiation have been exciting for the many people who have been involved with it. It has been a great experience to discover that there are not a lot of pat answers or pat programs that can be used to initiate. Those who have come to us seeking to become Catholic and who already have been living a deeply committed life of faith have challenged us to recognize that not everyone belongs in the catechumenate or its adapted process for baptized, uncatechized candidates. Developing a creative response to each person may at first seem difficult because of the time required from already overextended staffs and initiation teams. But if we believe that initiation is the work of the Spirit (Matthew 28), then we also have to believe that the people necessary to fulfill this work are in our assemblies; we just have to figure out who they are and invite them. It is the responsibility of all the baptized to initiate; it is our responsibility to envision new ways for them to fulfill their role as an initiating community.

The first challenge is to allow ourselves to be challenged by the people whom the Spirit brings to us as they seek the Lord through the witness of the community we call Catholic.

The second challenge comes to us from our experience and from the order itself. As the rites have been implemented in parish after parish, we have been blessed by generation after generation who have been excited by initiation ministry. The first generation, with little experience or idea of what it actually means to initiate, took the order and began to implement it. The second generation learned from them, and these two generations, along with a budding third generation, did extensive study, reflection and writing on their experience. These pioneers in initiation led many of us into a faithful understanding of the meaning of the initiation process. These first few generations constantly asked the questions: What are we doing? Why are we doing it?

There is always the danger of implementing the rites the way we do either because that is the way we have always done it or because that is the way they do it at a neighboring parish. The further we move away from the source of our initiation practices, from asking why we do what we do, the greater the danger that the implementation of the rites will become a program. When this happens, everyone (no matter where they are on their journey and no matter what clues the Spirit may be whispering to us) will be delivered to the door of the catechumenate, which then will probably become a program of instruction instead of a process of pastoral formation.

The challenge for initiation teams is to reflect, to study, to allow themselves to be challenged and to allow the vision of the order to be at the heart of the initiating parish. Again and again throughout the year, the initiation team and/or parish staff must ask, Why do we do what we do? If we answer honestly, this question will lead us into a deepened relationship with and appreciation for all the people whom the Spirit leads into our midst.

ENDNOTES

1. National Conference of Catholic Bishops, *Sharing the Light of Faith: National Catechetical Directory for Catholics of the United States* (Washington, D.C.: United States Catholic Conference, 1979), pp. 31 ff.

CHAPTER 2

Reception in Context: Historical, Theological and Pastoral Reflections

RITA FERRONE

EMERGING ECUMENISM

To understand the church's Rite of Reception of Baptized Christians into the Full Communion of the Catholic Church, it is necessary to view it in the context of the emergence of ecumenism as an important movement at the time of the Second Vatican Council. The existence of Christian churches and communities outside the visible communion of Rome is, of course, a very old phenomenon. Heretical churches (such as those of the Donatists, Monophysites and Arians) date from the fifth and sixth centuries. Separation of the Latin church from the churches of the East goes back to the eleventh century. In the West, the Protestant Reformation began in the sixteenth century. But an ecumenical movement involving most of the separated churches developed for the first time only in the twentieth century, and it was not until the second half of the twentieth century that the Catholic church formally adopted its present, positive attitude toward non-Catholic Christians.

Before the emergence of the ecumenical movement, the two categories used by Catholics to understand the status of non-Catholic Christians were heresy (holding and teaching false doctrine) and schism (causing and sustaining formal division from the church). Catholics believed that churches outside the communion of Rome were not truly the church of Jesus Christ and so should not exist. Any non-Catholic Christian confronted with the truth of Catholicism was obliged to convert and was held morally culpable if he or she failed to do so.[1] By present standards this judgment seems severe, but the fact that it does seem severe is testimony to the success of the ecumenical movement on all sides. The Catholic view was really not any more severe than the judgment of non-Catholics upon Catholics—nor, for that matter, of the various non-Catholic churches upon one another at various points in their histories.

The very manner in which "converts"[2] from other Christian churches were received into the Catholic communion reflected this uncompromising stance. Prior to the Second Vatican Council, anyone entering the Catholic church from one of the separated churches or communions had to make an abjuration of heresy and schism. The suspicion of the actual intentions and practices of Christians outside the pale of Rome was so great that baptized "converts" to Catholicism were routinely baptized again, conditionally, before receiving any other sacraments.[3] Thus Thomas Merton could write unblushingly of his baptism as an infant, according to the rites of the Church of England, that

> I don't think there was much power in the waters of the baptism I got . . . , to untwist the warping of my essential freedom, or loose me from the devils that hung like vampires on my soul.[4]

His comments may sound harsh to contemporary readers, but they harmonize well with the baptismal practices of the Catholic church in his time (*The Seven Storey Mountain* was published in 1948).

But by 1965, when the American president's youngest daughter, Luci Johnson, joined the Catholic church and was conditionally baptized, the Associated Press could report not only that "Episcopalian churchmen protested" but also that the Vatican itself called the baptism "regrettable."[5] The priest who performed the baptism defended his action, saying, "I did what thousands of other priests would have done,"[6] thus showing that at least in the United States, the new attitude had not reached the popular level. But a change had definitely taken place at the highest levels of the Catholic church. What had happened to bring this about?

CATHOLIC PARTICIPATION IN THE ECUMENICAL MOVEMENT: 1910 – SECOND VATICAN COUNCIL

On November 21, 1964, the fathers of the Second Vatican Council issued the *Decree on Ecumenism (Unitatis redintegratio)*, which begins by recognizing the existence of an ecumenical movement already in force:

> In recent times [the Lord of Ages] has begun to bestow more generously upon divided Christians remorse over their divisions and longing for unity. . . . Everywhere, large numbers have felt the impulse of this grace, and among our separated brethren also there increases from day to day a movement fostered by the grace of the Holy Spirit, for the restoration of unity among all Christians. . . . The sacred Council gladly notes all this.[7]

Indeed, an ecumenical movement that began among Protestants, Anglicans and Orthodox, and eventually engaged many Catholics, had been developing throughout the early part of the twentieth century.[8] As early as 1910 at the Edinburgh Missionary Conference, Anglicans and Protestants who met together voiced the need for church unity so that their missionary efforts could be more effective. Concern for unity also emerged from the Stockholm Life and Work Conference in 1925 and from the Faith and Order Conference at Lausanne in 1927.

Although invited, Catholics did not participate in these initial efforts, and Pope Pius XI's encyclical *Mortalium animos* (1928), on true religious unity, threw cold water over the prospect of Catholic participation in the ecumenical movement at this stage of its development. The encyclical stressed the necessity of accepting Christ's revelation completely, refused doctrinal compromise absolutely and rejected the notion that a federation of bodies holding different doctrines could be the church. These concerns were not unique to Catholics, however. The Orthodox delegation at Lausanne voiced similar concerns. Subsequent Faith and Order conferences (which Catholics did not attend) saw a deepening of denominational loyalties on all sides and a more formidable realization of doctrinal differences. Dialogue continued, but its course ran in the direction of more serious grappling with differences and rejection of superficial solutions.

Work toward church unity continued nonetheless in various ways, both within the Catholic church and outside it. Pius XI was deeply interested in the Orthodox churches; he issued 23 documents concerning them. He also worked with educational institutions and religious orders to increase Catholic understanding of and charity toward the Orthodox. Among non-Catholics the ecumenical movement continued to grow, and in 1948 the World Council of Churches (WCC) was formed from the International Missionary Council, Life and Work, and Faith and Order. By the time of the Second Vatican Council, 220 non-Catholic churches belonged to the WCC (notable exceptions being the Southern Baptist Convention and the Missouri Synod Lutheran Church). Catholic ecumenical institutes sprang up during the first half of the twentieth century in France, Germany, Holland and England. Father Yves Congar, OP, exerted a weighty influence on the Catholic ecumenical movement in France through his book *Divided Christendom*[9] (published in English in 1939), and Abbé Paul Couturier in 1932 popularized the idea of "spiritual ecumenism," which emphasizes the necessity of prayer in bringing about unity (the octave of prayer for church unity was begun by the Anglican church in 1908).

In his important encyclical on the church as the mystical body of Christ, *Mystici corporis Christi* (June 29, 1943), Pope Pius XII opened the door to ecumenism a bit further for Catholics by acknowledging that there are non-Catholic Christians who are "related to the Mystical Body of the Redeemer by some unconscious yearning or desire."[10]

His encyclical on sacred scripture, *Divine afflante Spiritu* (September 30, 1943), allowed scholars to use modern historical methods of biblical criticism, thus contributing to the possibility of developing greater common ground between Catholic and Protestant scripture scholars. Finally, in 1949 the Holy Office issued an instruction on the ecumenical movement, *Ecclesia Catholica*, which formally recognized the movement and endorsed Catholic participation in it.

Following this endorsement, the scope of ecumenical activity in the Catholic church increased. In 1952 (then Father) J.-G. M. Willebrands founded the Catholic Conference for Ecumenical Questions. The Catholic church sent official observers to the World Council of Churches in the late 50s and early 60s, and in 1960 Pope John XXIII established the Secretariat for the Promotion of the Unity of Christians under the leadership of Cardinal Augustin Bea. After the Council, this secretariat became a permanent (i.e., curial) institution.

Considerable groundwork for ecumenical cooperation was being laid in the biblical, patristic and historical scholarship of this period as well. Protestant and Catholic theologians began to talk to one another in a different spirit. Attitudes were changing; new ground was being broken. To give just a couple of illustrations: As early as 1958, theologian (then Father) Joseph Ratzinger, in addressing a pastoral congress in Vienna, could call it "obvious" that the category of heresy was inappropriate for the phenomenon of non-Catholic Christianity:

> There is no appropriate category in Catholic thought for the phenomenon of Protestantism today (one could say the same of the relationship to the separated churches of the East). It is obvious that the old category of "heresy" is no longer of any value. Heresy, for scripture and the early church, includes the idea of a personal decision against the unity of the church, and heresy's characteristic is *pertinacia*, the obstinacy of him who persists in his own private way. This, however, cannot be regarded as an appropriate description of the spiritual situation of the Protestant Christian. In the course of a now centuries-old history,

> Protestantism has made an important contribution to the
> realization of Christian faith, fulfilling a positive function
> in the development of the Christian message and, above
> all, often giving rise to a sincere and profound faith in
> the individual non-Catholic Christian, whose separation
> from the Catholic affirmation has nothing to do with the
> *pertinacia* characteristic of heresy.[11]

Another illustration from the late 1950s: When young Father Hans
Küng published his book on Karl Barth's doctrine of justification,[12]
he shocked his theological contemporaries by arguing convincingly
that the Reformed theologian Barth's position was within the compass
of Catholic doctrine. No one was more surprised than Barth
himself, whose anti-Catholic polemics were well known. Intrigued,
Barth agreed to write a foreword to the book, in which he assured
readers that Küng faithfully reported his theological position and—
obviously enjoying the daring nature of Küng's project—voiced a
devout hope that this event might be the harbinger of more truly ecumenical
dialogue between Protestants and Catholics.

> So then, like Noah I look forth from the window of my
> ark and salute your book as another clear omen that the
> days when Catholic and Protestant theologians would talk
> only against one another polemically or with one another
> in a spirit of noncommittal pacifism, but preferably not at
> all—that flood tide is, if not entirely abated, at least definitely
> receding.[13]

Catholic evaluation of the work was very positive and confirmed the
validity of Küng's insights,[14] though Father Karl Rahner's discussion
of the significance of the work regrets the fact that the Catholic
response was not more enthusiastic.

> Is not this agreement . . . amazing and something that can
> stir the heart and the spirit? Barth is not just anybody in
> Protestant theology. And he says: You give a hundred pages
> to my doctrine of justification; the presentation is excellent

and completely acceptable. And I have no difficulty in accepting what you put forward as the Catholic doctrine. Is this something easily imaginable? Or is it evidence of a development which strengthens our Christian hope, which God's commandments oblige us to have, that it is *possible* to advance in matters of the unity of the Christian faith?[15]

When the Second Vatican Council was convened, its deliberations took place in an atmosphere in which ecumenism held a very definite appeal as an authentic manifestation of the Spirit, calling all Christians to a deeper realization of the prayer of the Lord "that all may be one" (John 17:21). The non-Catholic observers at Vatican II were a visible reminder of the council's ecumenical purpose, and the views of these observers were heard, though indirectly. Many Catholics came to the council already committed to ecumenism. It is no wonder therefore that the council's *Constitution on the Church (Lumen gentium)*, its *Decree on Ecumenism (Unitatis redintegratio)* and its *Decree on Religious Liberty (Dignitatis humanae)* could voice for Catholics the world over a new perspective on churches and communions outside the visible communion of Rome.

Consider just a few of the assertions contained in the *Decree on Ecumenism*. The following are taken from paragraph 3:

> One cannot charge with the sin of separation those who at present are born into these communities [separated from the Catholic church].

> All who have been justified by faith in baptism are incorporated into Christ; they therefore have a right to be called Christians, and with good reason are accepted as brothers [sic] by the children of the Catholic church.

> Moreover, some, even very many, of the most significant elements and endowments which together go to build up and give life to the church itself, can exist outside the visible boundaries of the Catholic church: the written Word of God; the life of grace; faith, hope, and charity, with the

other interior gifts of the Holy Spirit, as well as visible elements.

The brethren divided from us also carry out many liturgical actions of the Christian religion. . . . these liturgical actions most certainly can truly engender a life of grace, and, one must say, can aptly give access to the communion of salvation.

Clearly, these assertions signal a shift in the official Catholic attitude. This new attitude, which is rightly called ecumenical, was accompanied by a commitment to dialogue and education, both of which have continued since the Council. Accordingly, Catholic thinking and practice concerning reception is informed by ecumenical convictions.

THE RITE OF RECEPTION

The Rite of Reception into the Full Communion of the Catholic Church, which was drafted in the late 1960s and first appeared in English in 1974, reflects the church's ecumenical attitude in many respects:

— An abjuration of heresy is no longer required of candidates (#479 U.S., 393 Can.).

— Conditional baptism is very narrowly circumscribed, and may not be celebrated publicly or with solemn rites (#480 U.S., 393 Can.).

— In view of the close relationship between the Catholic and the Orthodox churches, no rite of any kind is required for Orthodox candidates (#474 U.S., 388 Can.).

— The Rite of Reception may be celebrated within the Mass for Christian Unity (#487 U.S., 400 Can.).

— Triumphalism is to be avoided (#475.2 U.S., 389.2 Can.).

— Ecumenical sensitivity is allowed to dictate a more modest than usual approach to the celebration of the rite, limiting the participants to a few friends and family members (#475.2 U.S., 389.2 Can.).

—Anything that discounts the Christian identity of candidates and therefore equates them with catechumens is to be "absolutely avoided" (#477 U.S., 391 Can.).

—The readings chosen for the Rite of Reception, if the readings of the day or of the Mass for Christian Unity are not used (#501 U.S., 414 Can.), are passages well loved by all Christians, rather than controversial or "Roman" passages.

—The presider's invitation to the candidate's profession of faith (#490 U.S., 403 Can.) emphasizes pastoral and spiritual themes of free choice, thoughtful reflection and guidance by the Spirit.

—The profession of faith (#491 U.S., 404 Can.) contains no more than what is strictly necessary.

—If the candidate is accustomed to praying the doxology at the end of the Lord's Prayer, the doxology can be added when the rite is celebrated outside of Mass (#504 U.S., 417 Can.) (within Mass, of course, the doxology is included already).

The Rite of Reception is a humble rite, intentionally modest in its character and aims. What happens in the Rite of Reception is quite simply that an individual recites the Nicene Creed with the assembly (or, if it is celebrated in the Easter Vigil, renews baptismal promises with the assembly), makes a profession of Catholic faith and is then recognized by the church to be one with the Catholic community[16] (with a hand-laying[17] if confirmation is not to follow[18]). In most cases, confirmation is then celebrated.[19] Following confirmation, the presider takes both hands of the newly received into his to symbolize that person's acceptance.[20] Following the general intercessions, eucharist is celebrated.

Eucharist is of great importance to the Rite of Reception. The rite provides for the full use of the forms of the eucharist when it directs that the newly received and those who are with them may receive communion under both species (#498 U.S., 411 Can.).

The proper presider for this rite is the bishop (#481 U.S., 394 Can.) because of the importance of the episcopate to the nature of the Catholic church. Thus when the bishop lays his hand on the candidate, either in confirmation or in the act of acceptance, and when the newly received place their hands into the hands of the bishop, it becomes clear that they are engaged in a symbolic exchange with the entire local church, not only with their parish. When the bishop then presides at the eucharist that follows, the newly received candidates also have the benefit of seeing the church's norm of the eucharist most clearly realized.[21] Bishops may delegate the ministry of reception to priests, who then have the right to confirm (#481 U.S., 394 Can.) and normally would also preside at the eucharist. Yet the point should not be lost: The Rite of Reception brings the candidate into the whole of the Catholic church, with all its hierarchy and all its people, for hierarchy and laity together make up the communion of the church.[22]

To make a profession of faith is a serious matter, and its public nature is clear from the setting of the rite. Those who make any kind of profession of faith let the world know where they stand. In this case, the profession made by the baptized candidate establishes that this person has accepted and professes what the Catholic church "believes, teaches and proclaims to be revealed by God." The result of this profession is participation in the eucharistic communion of the Catholic church.[23] The Rite of Reception serves as gateway to the eucharistic communion of the Catholic faithful.

It is no accident, therefore, that the Rite of Reception normally takes place in the context of a eucharistic celebration. In the gathering of the faithful at the table of the eucharist, the church manifests itself most truly and fully as what it is — the body of Christ, head and members; the eschatological community of faith, witness and mission. The eucharist is the very center of the communion of the church. If there is any justifiable reason for separating reception from the eucharist, it would have to be very grave indeed, because the whole thrust of the reception of baptized Christians is toward its consummation in eucharistic communion. We should not be misled on this point by the fact that the rubrics allow for the possibility that reception might be separated from the eucharist. As always, having stated the norm first (#475.I U.S., 389.I Can.), with admirable clarity and forcefulness, the rite then gives direction to what should be done if for some reason the norm cannot be realized. This does not abolish or relativize the importance of the norm itself.

THEOLOGY OF COMMUNION

When the Rite of Reception first appeared in English, it bore the title "Rite of Reception of Baptized Christians into Full Communion *with* the Catholic Church" (emphasis added). A later translation by the International Commission on English in the Liturgy (ICEL) renders the title differently, not because the original title was changed (the Latin from which it is translated remains the same) but for greater accuracy in the English translation. The title now is rendered "Rite of Reception of Baptized Christians into *the* Full Communion *of* the Catholic Church" (emphasis added).

At first the difference in meaning between the two translations may seem negligible. But in fact, the difference is significant. The first: "Full communion with" suggests that what becomes full is the relationship between the individual and the Catholic church. This does happen in the process of reception, which is probably why so few people take note of the difference between "full communion with" and "the full communion of." The problem with this first formulation, however, is that it is imprecise. One can have a full relationship with a community that is only the bearer of part of the means that God has given to the church for salvation—which is not the kind of community that the Catholic church considers itself to be. In other words, one can enjoy communion with an objectively deficient or wounded community (say, for example one that has no Pope, no bishops, and no apostolic succession) and enjoy it to the full.

In the second formulation, however, "the full communion of" points to the existence in the Catholic church of an objective "full communion" which the individual candidate enters by means of reception. The focus shifts away from the quality of the relationship of the individual to the Catholic church and onto the Catholic church's integrity as a *full communion* into which the candidate is received. The full communion of the Catholic church includes the Pope and bishops, apostolic succession, a valid eucharist, and so on. Catholic doctrine considers these elements necessary to the identity of the church in an essential way; they are not inessential elements, options or frills. While some of them may also exist outside the full communion of the Catholic church, all of them are present within the Catholic church, making it possible for the fathers of Vatican II to say that the church of Jesus Christ "subsists in the Catholic church."[24] In other words, the Catholic church is "in the heart of an ecclesial reality that goes beyond its borders."[25]

It would be inadequate, however, to conceive of the full communion of the Catholic church solely or even primarily in terms of those things that are likely to be absent from other Christian churches and communities. The theological concept of communion is a broader and more fundamental term, as is evident from the way it is used in the New Testament and in the patristic period. The concept of communion has appeared in contemporary theological writing since the 1930s, and it appears with some frequency in the documents of Vatican II as a way to describe the nature of the church. In fact, the Extraordinary Synod of Bishops in 1985 asserted that communion was the crucial category voiced by Vatican II for understanding the church. In their 1992 letter on communion, the Congregation for the Doctrine of the Faith said

> The concept of communion (*koinonia*) . . . is very suitable for
> expressing the core of the mystery of the church and can
> certainly be a key for the renewal of Catholic ecclesiology.[26]

Over the past ten years, communion (*communio* or *communicatio* in Latin or *koinonia* in Greek) has become a term of central importance to ecumenical discussion as well.[27] Present in texts throughout the history of the ecumenical movement,[28] *koinonia* was chosen to be the overarching theme of the Fifth World Conference on Faith and Order (World Council of Churches), held in Santiago de Compostela, Spain, in August 1993—the first such world conference in thirty years. In sum, communion is a theological concept with a rich history and a wide present usage that cannot be reduced to a few controversial points.

In the New Testament, *koinonia* (fellowship or communion) is not a synonym for church and never refers simply to the local congregation[29] but is the actual sharing among Christians of life in the Spirit. This sharing is expressed in eucharistic communion understood both in its broadest sense as the common life of those who are brought together at the table of the Lord, as well as in the more narrow sense of its ritual expression in the liturgy. *Koinonia* is unanimity brought about by the Spirit;[30] it is participation in a new reality brought into existence by the redemption won by Christ. This reality consists of, first of all, a new relationship between humanity and God. Communion with God, lost because of the Fall, is restored to humanity by the death and resurrection of Jesus Christ.

J.-M. R. Tillard's masterwork on the notion of communion, *Church of Churches*, traces the beginnings of the church to the events of Pentecost, which reverse the effects of Babel and in symbolic fashion proclaim the dawn of a new era for the whole human race. He calls Pentecost the "theophany of the New Covenant"[31] and calls the pentecostal community "the manifestation, the *epiphaneia*, of the opening of the era of salvation."[32] The theme of this epiphany is reconciliation of all people with God through the blood of Christ, the apostles' preaching and the giving of the Spirit. Unlike the followers of Jesus during his earthly career (whose experience of a new reality could only be incomplete before the resurrection and the giving of the Spirit), the community of Pentecost reveals the universal significance of the gospel of God.

The second aspect of communion flows from the first and is inseparable from it. Reconciliation with God results in a genuinely restored relationship of charity, sharing and understanding among people. The grace of God in Christ Jesus gives us back our brothers and sisters who once were lost to us and to one another because of the terrible costs of sin. Communion builds of living stones one great temple, which is the dwelling place of the Spirit; it makes of living members one body, which is Christ.[33] This reality potentially includes all people, because it is won for all. But it begins to be realized first in the church, in the community of the baptized. Taking their cue from patristic writings, contemporary Catholic theologians stress the fact that this new relationship of reconciliation and Spirit-filled life is found quintessentially in the eucharistic community, where communion is realized sacramentally as well as in the lives of the believers.

Sadly, the beautiful realities spoken about in articulating the essence of the church as communion may sound more like a vision we glimpse from afar rather than a solid and sure foundation near at hand. What are we to say when even the most devoted believers among us cry out, "Where is my church? Where are my brothers and sisters?" We cannot point to the pope in Rome or the bishops or the texts of sacred scripture and expect it to suffice. If our parishes and dioceses are not places where charity and love prevail, where we are brothers and sisters to one another in truth and in faith, God's gift of communion will remain obscured. That is why the *Decree on Ecumenism* very wisely cautions that the first order of business for those who work for church unity must be the purification of our own church body.[34] The increase of our obedience to Christ, our singleness of heart and our oneness in charity are the necessary prerequisites for disposing ourselves to show forth the gift of communion.

THE EXPERIENCE OF RECEPTION

The *Decree on Ecumenism (Unitatis redintegratio)* and the subsequent *Directory on Ecumenism* both state that although ecumenism and reception are by nature distinct, they are not opposed. The Decree goes on to say that "both proceed from the marvelous ways of God."[35] Neither document spells out how the two are distinct, why they are not opposed or what exactly these marvelous ways of God are, but the answers to these questions are not hard to discover.

The two are distinct in three ways: First, ecumenism concerns groups of people, whereas reception concerns individuals. Second, ecumenism involves dialogue among church bodies, none of which seek to become one of the others. Reception involves an individual developing an "inner adherence to the church" (#477 U.S., 391 Can.); that is to say, the candidate becomes Catholic.[36] Finally, ecumenism aims toward a future church that will not be identical to any one of the church bodies that now exist; the aim is to gather into one all the traditions and institutions that are truly the work of Christ's Spirit. Its time frame is necessarily very long. Reception, however, has the more limited aim of fully incorporating an individual into an existing church body. The time it takes to accomplish reception may be very short indeed.

There is no opposition between ecumenism and reception into the Catholic church, first, because the candidate is being received into a church that is irrevocably committed to working for the unity of Christians. Second, reception is carried on in a spirit of respect for the freedom and the Christian identity of the candidate for reception, both of which are key elements of ecumenism. Third, the Catholic church, both in its work for Christian unity and in the process of receiving persons into its communion, seeks to respond to the mystery of God's call. The Catholic church recognizes that the grace of God is at work in both processes and that God's grace does not lead to conflict and opposition but to unity and peace.

The last question—What are these marvelous ways of God?— invites us to take a closer look at the experience of reception as a potential source for theological reflection. The literature on ecumenism is voluminous, naturally, because ecumenical dialogue is an industry of educated experts. For every embrace the Pope gives the Archbishop of Canterbury or the Patriarch of Constantinople, there are pounds of paper anticipating it beforehand and reflecting on it afterward.

But there is almost no literature—theological or otherwise—on the phenomenon of reception into the full communion of the Catholic church as it has existed since the Second Vatican Council. "Convert" literature that dates from the era prior to Vatican II is of very limited usefulness because we are in a different situation today. But nothing has risen to take its place.

The absence of sustained theological reflection on our new situation is an unfortunate lapse. Some Catholics are still wedded to a triumphalistic view of reception that regards Rome as little less than the heavenly Jerusalem. Others would have us believe that reception is little better than "sheep stealing" from other Christian flocks and would not happen any more if a truly ecumenical spirit took hold in the church. Neither of these views does justice to a Catholic understanding of the nature of the church, however, and both take less than seriously the actual experience of candidates and the communities that receive them.

Three Movements

If one did take these things into account, however, one would see at least three movements that are normally part of the process of reception, each of which may be viewed without prejudice to the work of ecumenism as particular expressions of the marvelous ways of God.

First is the apprehension of distinct gifts in Catholicism. The candidate has been attracted to this community and persists in seeking reception for some reason. The impulse may or may not be very well founded or thoughtful at first, but if it is not, it may become so in the process of sharing, learning and discernment that necessarily follows an initial approach to the local church. Through the process of coming into the full communion of the Catholic church, candidates normally become better able to discern and to name the particular gifts that they have come to appreciate and value in this communion. The objective awareness of Catholicism's particular identity plays an important role in formulating a subjective response and commitment.

The candidate's perception of the special qualities of the Catholic tradition is a gift to the church, refreshing our own awareness of the riches of our communion even as the candidate may challenge us to be more true to our truest selves.

Second, to the extent that candidates have been formed in another Christian tradition, they bring with them the spiritual riches of that tradition. A keen sensitivity to scripture, strong musical traditions, an awareness of the need for witnessing, social commitment based on the gospel, and various elements of faith and piety are some examples of religious heritage that candidates may bring with them. Such gifts strengthen and enrich the Catholic communities that receive these candidates. Certain candidates may at first be eager to retreat from or shed their previous denominational identity, but a complete metamorphosis can rarely be accomplished and probably should not happen anyway. Someone who has been formed in another Christian tradition will eventually find that the virtues of that tradition will emerge in their new Catholic identity. Good Catholics will welcome this and not suppress it, because in a modest way it increases the catholicity of the Catholic church. While this is no substitute for the work of uniting with other church bodies in their entirety, it is nonetheless a way in which a healthy ecumenical regard for aspects of authentic Christianity that are found outside the Catholic church is transposed into a personal key. It is a rare candidate indeed who does not come bearing gifts.

Third, part of the mystery involved in people coming to be received into the full communion of the Catholic church is that it is and must be linked with the call to deeper holiness of life, the call to ongoing conversion that belongs to all the faithful. If reception is nothing more than a paper transfer, a change of membership from one bureaucratic organization to another, there is no justification for it. The Rite of Reception assumes that the candidate is responding to the call of God. That is why it is a liturgical rite and cannot be done through the mail. If the candidate is responding to a call from God, that response must take on the quality of a renewed conversion of heart to the One who calls us. Anything less does no honor to the separated churches and communions from which the candidates come and only perpetuates the fiction that each individual merely chooses the church that best suits him or her at that time.

The call to holiness, to conversion, must be considered the first priority of all the activity surrounding reception. It reigns over and, if necessary, supersedes the other two movements we have just considered, because a just appreciation of the gifts of Catholicism and a true willingness to share from the storehouse of one's spiritual history demand a chastened self-awareness, humility, patience and all the spiritual gifts that come from God. Only our ongoing conversion to the crucified and risen Lord will set our feet on the right path and keep us on it.

CONCLUSION

The Rite of Reception can truly be called an invention of our day, created in the context of an ecumenical situation unprecedented in the history of the church. Yet in this new situation, in this new rite, the ancient language of creed and embrace and eucharist continues to speak of what the Catholic church is most essentially and of what it means to belong to this church.

The context of reception is complex: Reception exists in a situation of real divisions among churches. It exists against the background of our hope of achieving greater unity among all Christians. And it exists as a reflection and expression of a Catholic understanding of the nature of the church itself. Each of these aspects of the context of reception contributes to our understanding of the rite itself and of the reality it celebrates.

1. Karl Rahner, "Some Remarks on the Question of Conversions," trans. Karl-H. Kruger, *Theological Investigations Vol. 5: Later Writings* (Baltimore: Helicon Press, 1966), 315 ff.

2. The U.S. National Statutes for the Catechumenate (1988) forbid us to call baptized Christians who enter into the full communion of the Catholic church "converts." The term "convert" is to be strictly reserved for those who pass from unbelief to Christian faith (See appendix III, *National Statutes* #2, U.S. only).

3. Often, having received forgiveness of all sins in baptism, the "converts" then went immediately to have them forgiven again in the sacrament of penance.

4. Thomas Merton, *The Seven Storey Mountain* (New York: Harcourt, Brace and Company, Inc., 1948), 11.

5. *The World in 1965: History as We Lived It* (n.p.: The Associated Press, 1966), 136.

6. Ibid.

7. *Decree on Ecumenism,* #1.

8. Facts about the history of the ecumenical movement, unless otherwise noted, are taken from the *New Catholic Encyclopedia* and *Sacramentum Mundi.*

9. *Chrétiens Désunis* (1937); *Divided Christendom: a Catholic Study of the Problem of Reunion,* trans. M. A. Bousfield (London: G. Bles, 1939).

10. Eric John, ed., *The Popes: A Concise Biographical History* (New York: Hawthorne Books, 1964), 468.

11. Joseph Cardinal Ratzinger, *The Meaning of Christian Brotherhood,* 2d English ed. (San Francisco: Ignatius Press, 1993), 87–88.

12. Hans Küng, *Justification: The Doctrine of Karl Barth and a Catholic Reflection,* trans. Thomas Collins, Edmund E. Tolk and David Granskou (New York: Thomas Nelson and Sons, 1964).

13. Karl Barth, "A Letter to the Author" (January 31, 1957), *Justification: The Doctrine of Karl Barth and a Catholic Reflection,* by Hans Küng, trans. Thomas Collins, Edmund E. Tolk and David Granskou (New York: Thomas Nelson and Sons, 1964), xxi.

14. See Küng's preface to the English edition, p. xi, in which he quotes J. L. Witte, professor of controversial theology at the Pontifical Gregorian University (from *Münchner Theologische Zeitschrift* 10 [1959], 38 ff.): "Already an express Catholic consensus has become apparent insofar as all Catholic reviews, with all their criticism of details, are agreed that the elements of justification as developed in the second part of this book do present a theological interpretation which is, at least, a possible one in the Catholic Church." See also Karl Rahner, "Questions of Controversial Theology on Justification" in *Theological Investigations, Volume IV: More Recent Writings,* trans. Kevin Smyth (Baltimore: Helicon Press, 1966), 190, footnote 2.

15. Karl Rahner, "Questions of Controversial Theology on Justification," 193.

16. The formula for this Act of Reception (#492 U.S., 405 Can.) is inspired by the rite of the Jacobite Syrians (see H. Denzinger, *Ritus Orientalium i*, 466).

17. This is an ancient gesture used when reconciling schismatics and apostates.

18. When confirmation follows, the hand-laying is omitted (#492 U.S., 405 Can.).

19. Any candidates who have not been validly confirmed are confirmed before they are brought to the table. The vast majority of candidates must be confirmed. Some exceptions are the Old Catholics, members of the Polish National Catholic Church and the Society of Pius X—a tiny minority of all possible candidates.

20. The Rite of Reception preserves in a modernized form the bishop's kiss that we see in the *Apostolic Tradition of Hippolytus* after the second postbaptismal anointing. (The committee that drafted the rite notes the origins of this gesture in *Schemata, n. 290 De Rituali*, n. 28, April 21, 1968 [ICEL Archives, Washington, D.C.] 7, note 10.) This kiss is distinct from the sign of peace shared with the whole assembly. The way in which the Rite of Reception has modernized the gesture— by having the presider take the hands of the newly received—is left open to adaptation with the permission of local authorities (#495 U.S., 408 Can.).

21. "Concerning the eucharist, the Council reasserted that its normal performance is to be seen in that of the bishop presiding within an event that concretely expresses the full involvement of the whole local church.... The norm means not that the bishop must preside at every Mass, even if this were possible. It does mean, however, that in both theory and practice the eucharist is never to be regarded as anything less than an act of the whole church, head and members, and that this *norm* to some extent must always be achieved, even when the chief pastor of the local church does not himself preside." Aidan Kavanagh, *The Shape of Baptism* (New York: Pueblo Publishing Co., 1978), 107.

22. "'[T]he communion of the churches and the collegiality of the bishops is based on the more fundamental communion which is the church, the people of God itself.... as the council uses the phrase, the people of God does not mean the laity, for example, or the rank and file, as distinct from 'the official church,' let alone in contrast to it. It means the organic and structured whole of the church." . .. Walter Kasper, *Theology and Church*, trans. Margaret Kohl (New York: Crossroad, 1989), 161–162.

23. Although confirmation usually follows the profession of faith, it is not the "high point" or symbolic center of the liturgy. Both reception and confirmation are oriented toward the eucharist, which is the culmination of the whole initiation process.

24. *Decree on Ecumenism, 4; Dogmatic Constitution on the Church, 8.*

25. J.-M. R. Tillard, *Church of Churches: The Ecclesiology of Communion*, trans. R. C. De Peaux (Collegeville: The Liturgical Press, 1992), 316.

26. "Some Aspects of the Church Understood as Communion," *Origins* 12, no. 7 (June 25, 1992): 108. Although the letter is signed by Cardinal Ratzinger as prefect of the Congregation, and Archbishop Bovone as secretary, it is produced by the Congregation itself.

27. For an insightful discussion of the various uses of this term in ecumenical dialogue, see George Vandervelde, "Koinonia Ecclesiology—Ecumenical Breakthrough?" *One in Christ* 29 (1993).

28. Lorelei F. Fuchs SA, "Koinonia: Text and Context for the Church," *Ecumenical Trends* 22, 2 (Feb. 1993): 8–11.

29. J. Schattenmann, "Koinonia" in *The New International Dictionary of New Testament Theology*, vol. I, ed. Colin Brown (Zondervan: Grand Rapids, 1975), 643.

30. Ibid., 642.

31. Tillard, *Church of Churches*, 10.

32. Ibid., 8.

33. Ibid., 22–23.

34. "In ecumenical work, Catholics must assuredly be concerned for their separated brethren.... But their primary duty is to make a careful and honest appraisal of whatever needs to be renewed and done in the Catholic household itself ... For although the Catholic Church has been endowed with all divinely revealed truth and with all means of grace, yet its members fail to live by them with the fervor that they should ... Every Catholic must therefore aim at Christian perfection and, each according to his station, play his part, that the Church, which bears in her own body the humility and dying of Jesus, may daily be more purified and renewed, against the day when Christ will present her to himself, in all her glory ..." *Decree on Ecumenism*, 4.

35. *Decree on Ecumenism*, 4: "... it is evident that the work of preparing and reconciling those individuals who wish for full Catholic communion is of its nature distinct from ecumenical action. But there is no opposition between the two ..." See also the 1993 *Directory for Ecumenism*, 99.

36. "Fully incorporated into the church are those who, possessing the Spirit of Christ, accept all the means of salvation given to the church together with her entire organization, and who ... by the bonds constituted by the profession of faith, the sacraments, ecclesial government, and communion—are joined in the visible structure of the church of Christ, who rules her through the Supreme Pontiff and the bishops" (*Dogmatic Constitution on the Church*, 14).

CHAPTER THREE

Reconciliation as Second Baptism

JOSEPH A. FAVAZZA

Tertullian, writing around 203 CE, spoke of the experience of ecclesial reconciliation as a *paenitentia secunda*, a second penance. His turn of phrase reveals an insight of profound importance for second- and third-century Christian churches: The effects of baptism and reconciliation were interchangeable. Both cleansed one of sin through penance and admitted one to the eucharistic table. Both were unrepeatable. For the Christian alienated from the community (and so from God) through sin after baptism, there was but one more opportunity to come into the loving embrace of the church. Transposing Tertullian's phrase (but not his meaning), one can speak of the experience of reconciliation as a second baptism.

While we can be thankful that the evolving discipline of the church led us away from the practice of unrepeatable ecclesial reconciliation, perhaps it is this very evolution that has led to a loss of the family resemblance between baptism and reconciliation. If reconciliation is repeatable, we reason, it must be either a radically different animal from, or radically less powerful than, baptism. Herein is found the purpose of this chapter: to discover and rediscover the "second baptism" of reconciliation as inherent to the initiation journey, especially for those who have already celebrated the "first penance" of baptism.

This task is undertaken in three parts. I will begin with some observations on contemporary pastoral practice and then explore how a similar pastoral challenge was resolved by the church during the formative third century. Finally, I will attempt to articulate a sound theological foundation to inform renewed pastoral practice.

INITIATING THE ALREADY BAPTIZED: CONTEMPORARY PASTORAL PRACTICE

I have often thought that baptized Christians who present themselves for initiation into the Catholic community are embodied seasons of Advent: Something wonderful has already happened, yet we await it afresh. They are the "already but not yet," incarnated reminders of a world full of grace and yearning for fulfillment.

They come with their unique stories of past connections with other church communities. For some, it is a relationship full of vitality and non-regretting memory. For others, it is a name-only experience, whereby one could confidently state they were Methodist or Baptist or even Catholic while having no real idea what that meant. Outward status was intact, while inward conversion remained unawakened.

Like Advent itself, these persons provide the church with a pastoral opportunity (which is another way of saying their presence in our midst is still a pastoral conundrum!). What do we do with them? The *Rite of Christian Initiation of Adults* specifies only that the process of initiation should be suited to the particular situation of each candidate (#477–478 U.S., 391 Can.). There is pastoral leeway here; yet, how each local community responds to the situation of these Advent-likened souls reveals basic ecclesiological assumptions. Allow me to explore the two most common responses from our recent past.

CONDITIONAL BAPTISM AND CONDITIONAL "CATECHUMENIZATION"

Prior to the Second Vatican Council, baptized Christians presenting themselves for full initiation more often than not were conditionally baptized. The official reason often cited for this action was reasonable doubt about the "form" of their baptism. In other words, the rite used to baptize was lacking something canonically essential to make the baptism valid. Just as in the case of Catholic Christians who marry outside the church and are later able to obtain annulments based on a "defect" in the form of their marriage, so pastors were able to baptize conditionally just about all Christians who presented themselves for initiation based on a "defect" in the form of their baptism. It was the pastorally simple thing to do.

From an ecclesial perspective, wholesale conditional baptism reveals a basic ecclesiological assumption: In order to break through the well-insulated boundary of the "One, True Church," one must abide by the rites of that church and no other. This demonstrates not only a powerfully confident trust in the efficacy of one's rituals but an exaggerated mistrust in the rituals of outside groups. Obviously, this expressed the highly institutional ecclesial model that defined the Catholic community before the Second Vatican Council.

Due to the Council's commitment both to make ecumenism a guiding principle in the renewal of the church and to restore the catechumenate, conditional baptism happily has become an extraordinary procedure.[1] Instead of rebaptizing these Christians, however, we often invite them virtually to forget about their baptism and to take the same initiatory journey through the catechumenate that unbaptized persons do. We celebrate rites particular to them, while all the other aspects of their formation are identical to the unbaptized. In the language of pop culture, we talk the talk ("We recognize the validity of your Christian baptism . . ."), but we don't always walk the walk ("but it made little difference, so get in line with all the unbaptized"). We dare not rebaptize, but sometimes we send a not-so-implicit message that their baptism counts for little.[2]

Here the basic ecclesiological assumption at work is that the church, as a community of faith in which the living Savior is made present through word and sacrament, is best modeled in the initiation rites for unbaptized persons. We trust the order of Christian initiation to animate and respect the conversion process, but we may not trust the other rites provided by the church to do the same. Even though the ritual text itself is explicit that "the baptized Christian is to receive both doctrinal and spiritual preparation, adapted to individual pastoral requirements" (#477 U.S., 391 Can.) and that "discernment should be made regarding the length of catechetical formation required for each individual candidate" (#478, U.S. only), we stretch the parish's catechumenate to fit as many pastoral opportunities as possible. We extend it to both catechized and uncatechized alike, to those already initiated into other ecclesial communities and those who have already been initiated as Catholic Christians. This presents at least the appearance of "one size fits all" when it comes to initiation.

A MODEST PROPOSAL:
RECONCILE THE ALREADY BAPTIZED

Allow me to propose one more answer to the question posed by the presence of the already baptized. While perhaps foreign to the ears of contemporaries, it is an answer completely conventional in the early church, as we shall soon see. What do we do with the already baptized? Reconcile them!

During the past few years, I have had the opportunity to hear from a number of catechumenate directors about how sacramental reconciliation is celebrated with baptized Christians. As one might imagine, the various ways are as diverse and unique as the church itself. I will summarize those elements of pastoral practice which appear with the most frequency.

For many inquirers, "confession" is a big issue. Therefore, adequate time is spent during the precatechumenate period answering questions about the sacramental practice of reconciliation. Usually this is done without reference to individual life situations; only enough information to calm fears and address questions is provided. In some cases, inquirers are given the message, subtle or otherwise, that reconciliation is one of those "Catholic suitcases" one just has to take along if one is to make the journey. It may be heavy, but it won't break your back.

In many cases, reconciliation does not emerge again (or as one catechumenate director said: "Rear its ugly head"!) until the period of purification and enlightenment, usually during the Lenten season, when candidates are within weeks of reception. Some parishes celebrate the suggested penitential rite for candidates (#459–472, U.S. only) on the Second Sunday of Lent. In preparation for this celebration or as part of the mystagogical reflection afterward, the topic of sacramental reconciliation is addressed. Candidates are instructed on how to celebrate the rite and are encouraged either to make an appointment with a priest or come to the parish penance service, which most parishes celebrate sometime during Lent.[3] In a few instances, a penance service is celebrated only for candidates, sponsors and their families. Of course, sponsors are strongly encouraged to talk privately with candidates about reconciliation, especially in cases where the candidate shows signs of nervousness or anxiety.

Most directors report that candidates are not pressured to celebrate reconciliation. Each candidate makes this decision "according to his or her own conscience" (#482 U.S., 395 Can.). The ideal of following one's conscience is sometimes interpreted to mean, however, that celebrating reconciliation is an entirely personal decision on the part of the candidate, with no input or direction by those entrusted with his or her formation. For an initiation team anxious "that no greater burden than necessary" (#473 U.S., 387 Can.) be placed on the candidate, and for a candidate anxious about celebrating reconciliation anyway, this makes for a happy coincidence. In fact, most directors did not know if all the candidates for reception at their parish celebrated sacramental reconciliation prior to their initiation.

Certainly, there are both more and less pastorally sensitive exceptions to the elements of practice just described. But if this comes close to the mark in even a few parishes, there is work to be done. To segregate the reception of the already baptized from a meaningful process of reconciliation is like building four walls and a roof and calling it a house. It will look like a house in relation to other houses, but something inherent is missing. For the sake of gaining a better understanding of why such a compartmentalized approach occurs, let's explore two fundamental assumptions that underlie the pastoral practice.

Assumption 1: Reconciliation Is External to the Initiation Process

There appears to be widespread pastoral amnesia about the fundamental familial relationship between initiation and reconciliation in the formation process. One sees this every time reconciliation is introduced as an external element to the initiation process rather than as an intrinsic part of the process itself. Little or no connection is made between the experience of reconciliation and the life experiences of the candidates. The catechetical and pastoral wisdom that leads us to connect ritual with experience in the initiation process, to connect the story of the community with the story of the individual, is left by the door of the reconciliation room.

Some readers might immediately object and say that comparing initiation to reconciliation is like comparing apples to oranges. After all, initiation is public and communal, whereas reconciliation is private and personal. This is exactly the point. We bring an anorectic practice of reconciliation to the sumptuous meal of initiation and draw the conclusion that the two are disconnected. Forgotten is the essential truth that reconciliation, like initiation, is conversion into, commitment to, and celebration in, community. But more on this later.

From a pastoral perspective, I suspect reconciliation is being celebrated with candidates without the "permission" of the sacramental rite, such as in the empathetic and active listening by sponsors and team members as a candidate struggles to make sense of existential alienation and/or broken relationships. In fact, our parish communities are filled with "lay confessors," people who by their compassion and wholeness (holiness) invite others to share their struggle and pain with them. The challenge here is less to start doing something new to celebrate reconciliation and more to connect what is already happening to the sacramental experience of reconciliation throughout the formation process.

Assumption 2: Ritual Reconciliation Is Meaningless

One of the side effects of the renewal of the Second Vatican Council is increased personal responsibility in the formation of conscience. No longer is it enough to listen to what the church teaches and then believe it. One is asked to become personally engaged and to make sometimes difficult and painful decisions of conscience. In short, we have been asked to become less like children, who rely on parents for all their direction, and more like responsible and free adults. To see the effects of this, one need only look at the non-acceptance of the church's teaching regarding artificially regulating birth by a large majority of Roman Catholics in the U.S. and Canada.

From an anthropological and sociological perspective, the more a community internalizes its religious values and experiences, the less it relies on its rituals that are perceived as upholding a value system that does not account for the plurality in individual decisions of conscience.[4] The precipitous drop in the number of Catholics who actually celebrate sacramental reconciliation may be an indication of an overall crisis of doubt about the efficacy of our rituals, especially our rites of purification or healing. To find Catholics who no longer find any meaning in the church's rite of reconciliation or who perceive it as magic (yes, even among initiation teams and the clergy) is consistent with the difficult task of growing up. We are still discovering new ways of ritually celebrating our internal experience.

Tied to this has been the explicit intention of church leaders to restrict the celebration of the most communal form of the *Rite of Penance* (Form III: Rite for Reconciliation of Several Penitents with General Confession and Absolution). It is difficult to balance personal conversion with the essential communal nature of reconciliation when local communities are constrained, except in extraordinary situations, to celebrate sacramental reconciliation only in its least communal forms. While Form II (Rite for Reconciliation of Several Penitents with Individual Confession and Absolution) moves us in this direction, it is a hybrid of Form I (Rite for Reconciliation of Individual Penitents) and Form III rather than a distinctly communal form of the rite.[5]

Given the current ritual impasse of the sacrament, no wonder many communities are experimenting with more communal expressions of the rite, including pastoral variations of a restored order of penitents.[6] In the end, these rites may bring about a renewed confidence in the efficacy of our rituals of reconciliation. They respect the process of conversion, they invite the unfolding of a variety of ministerial roles, and, most importantly, they make present the limitless and loving embrace of the living God in the assembled community.

RECONCILING THE ALREADY BAPTIZED: RELEARNING PAST LESSONS

The challenging question of what to do with those baptized into another Christian community is one that other generations have had to answer. Perhaps no answer is as dramatic as the one that emerged from the third-century disagreement between the bishop of Rome, Stephen, and his North African colleague, Cyprian of Carthage — both strong, uncompromising characters. Because there are lessons here to inform contemporary practice, it is worth exploring the controversy and the solution that emerged.[7]

THE PROBLEM

In late 249, the emperor Decius decreed that all citizens of the Roman Empire were to offer sacrifice to the traditional Roman gods in honor of a decisive military victory. By the end of the next year, Christian communities all across the empire were undergoing great spiritual turmoil and social upheaval as their members were faced with this life-threatening decision.

Some, like Cyprian, were able to go underground in the hope that the persecution would end before they could be discovered. Others were forced to make a choice: Refuse to offer sacrifice and risk imprisonment and death, acquiesce and perform temple sacrifice, or obtain by bribery a certificate claiming one had offered sacrifice when in fact one had not. Those choosing the latter two options, known as the *lapsi* (lapsed), automatically were excluded from the community through their apostasy.

After the persecution ended in the spring of 251, the bishops of North Africa, led by Cyprian, convened in council to decide how to handle the pastoral challenge presented by the *lapsi:* By what means could they hope to be reconciled to the Christian community? It was decided that those who had obtained certificates and who already had begun acts of repentance were to be reconciled immediately and readmitted to the eucharist by the laying on of the hand by the bishop. However, those who had actually made a sacrifice to the gods were to continue in the order of penitents and be reconciled only in danger of death.

This decision raised the ire of both the rigorists, who thought the bishops were being too lenient with the first group, and the laxists, who thought the bishops were being much too harsh against the second group. (Even in the third century, bishops could not please all of the people all of the time!)

At the same time, trouble was developing in Rome. At the end of the persecution, Cornelius was elected bishop to replace Fabian, who had died a martyr's death. All extant evidence points to the validity of the election, which was subsequently confirmed by the African bishops. However, for reasons which remain unclear, a dissenting group was formed, led by the presbyter Novatian. He proceeded to establish a rival communion and the result was schism.

The disagreement between the radically rigorous Novatian and the more moderate Cornelius became focused on their policy regarding the *lapsi.* Cornelius took the position of Cyprian and the African bishops. Novatian, however, claimed that such a policy compromised the purity of the church; therefore, the *lapsi* were never to be readmitted to communion, even if they undertook the most severe penance or were in danger of death. The church could provide care and solicitude, but never the "fatal poison of hasty reconciliation."[8]

We can only imagine Novatian's displeasure when, in 253, the African bishops amended their previous policy and encouraged individual bishops to reconcile those who had sacrificed, in order to give them every spiritual advantage in the face of a possible renewed persecution. This policy was perceived by the rigorist camp as yet another victory by the laxists, made even more pervasive when Cornelius adopted it a few weeks later for the Roman church. After Cornelius died in exile, his short-lived successor, Lucius, also confirmed the policy. In May of the following year, Stephen was elected bishop of Rome and the controversy took a new twist.

Stephen was a man of strong principles and apparent contradictions. On the one hand, he refused the plea of Cyprian and other bishops to intervene and remove the bishop of Arles, who had taken Novatian's harsh position and was refusing to reconcile the *lapsi*. On the other hand, he supported the reinstatement of two Spanish bishops who had been removed for their alleged apostasy during the persecution. Such controversial stands led to vehement disagreement between Stephen and Cyprian and set the stage for their most serious and famous disagreement of all: the issue of rebaptism.

THE SOLUTION

The question about what to do with the *lapsi* after the Decian persecution eventually led to schism. The rival communions, such as the one formed by the rigorist Novatian, spread to all parts of the Christian world. This inevitably led to yet another question: What to do with those persons who had followed such groups into schism, were initiated through baptism and eucharist, and now wished to return to orthodoxy? In other words, what to do with those Christians who were baptized into another Christian community and now wished to join the "Catholic" (as per Cyprian) church? If one leaves aside the third-century interpretation of heresy and looks only at the pastoral challenge presented by such persons, it is the same question being asked today. Cyprian proposed one answer; Stephen proposed another.[9]

Cyprian upheld the tradition of the African church: All those who had been baptized into a schismatic community had to be rebaptized upon entering the Catholic communion.[10] His position turned on his ecclesiology: The Catholic church is the only one, true church, outside of which salvation is not possible. The boundaries of the church are very clearly delineated; therefore, ritual actions taken outside these boundaries are ineffective. Any recognition of the legitimacy of rival communities was perceived by Cyprian as a threat to the unique status of the Catholic communion.

Cyprian's position must be understood in the context of the great social upheaval brought about by the Decian persecution and Cyprian's attempt to affirm the efficacy of his own rituals in the face of the *lapsi* controversy. From his viewpoint, the rebaptism of previously baptized Christians was not even a question. Because their first baptism was useless, they needed the baptism of the Catholic church in order to be saved. (While extreme, Cyprian's position may be likened to the practice of conditional baptism prior to the Second Vatican Council, to which Rita Ferrone referred in chapter 2.)

In contrast, Stephen upheld the validity of the baptisms of those initiated by schismatic groups. Whereas Cyprian was unyielding in his negative judgment on the rituals of competing Christian communities, Stephen's position appears more nuanced. He believed that the church of Christ and the possibility of salvation was more expansive than a single communion. He accepted the baptism of Novatian and his group of rigorists. He tolerated the bishop who refused to grant reconciliation to the *lapsi*. He excommunicated, and was excommunicated by, the African and Asian bishops without fearing the loss of salvation for those in these churches or in his own. Clearly, he viewed Christian communities not in communion with Rome both as candidates for salvation and as having efficacious rituals.

Given this ecclesiology, what is to be done with previously baptized Christians who seek admission to the Catholic church? Stephen's answer is simple: Lay the bishop's hand on them; reconcile them and admit them to the eucharist. Do this not just because the baptisms of competing communities are valid, at least in the eyes of Christ, but especially because of the "super"-efficacy of the Catholic rite of reconciliation. It works—and nothing more is needed.

Granted, Stephen's position on reconciliation is inseparable from his position upholding the absolute authority of bishops, especially the successor of Peter. Also, Stephen might well have been playing politics with the followers of Novatian ("I'll recognize your baptism if you will trust your salvation to the efficacy of our rite of reconciliation"). Yet it is Stephen's position that wins the day: Those coming from other Christian communities need not be rebaptized nor even reduced again to the status of catechumens. They need only to be reconciled.

INITIATION AND RECONCILIATION: THEOLOGICAL FOUNDATIONS FOR THE FUTURE

I have offered some observations about contemporary pastoral practice and have explored how the early church answered the pastoral challenge of baptized Christians seeking initiation into the Catholic community. It is now time to establish the theological foundation upon which can be grounded the hope for a future family reunion between baptism and reconciliation in the pastoral life of the church.

Some in our communities view the church's ritual celebrations as unchanging possessions central to the rich heritage of tradition. Yet by their very purpose, sacraments are living, changing traditions, not things to be protected like so many rare documents in the Vatican Museum. Successive generations have the never-ending task of restoring, reforming and renewing our rituals to incarnate the very principle upon which Christianity as a religion is based: God became one like us and continues to be present and recognizable in everything human. Our desires, actions, experiences and hopes, indeed all human realities, are God-charged. Sacraments are efficacious moments that make God present at the very core of human longings for fulfillment.

Initiation and reconciliation are intensely human events. Both point to the simple and often forgotten fact that being most deeply human is being in relationship. If we are made in God's image, and if God is love, so we also are called out of our solitary lives and are invited into the lives of others, all in love. The deep longings in each of us to belong, to connect with others beyond the point where our flesh ends, to be at peace and in communion with ourselves, others and the world, are not just flights of fancy in a hard and desperate world. No, they endure as what is most real about us. All human experiences of initiation and reconciliation, from the simplest to the most profound, fulfill this longing of our truest selves.

As sacraments of the church, initiation and reconciliation are celebrations by the community to create community. They are Easter moments which expose the unnaturalness of isolation and alienation, fear and bondage, sin and death. What is most real and most deeply human is all that leads us to relationship and healing, freedom and community, forgiveness and life. In a word, it is all that leads us to God, made present in the journey of Jesus, who destroyed death and restored life. Resurrection is celebrated when the community gathers to tell the story of life's power over death; this action fulfills once more the intense human desire for intimate communion with God made present in a common meal. Those initiated and reconciled into community know they have passed from death to life when they eat and drink at the Lord's table.

From this perspective, sacramental initiation and reconciliation are intrinsically connected as source and summit of a deeper humanity. They are paradigms of the life of relationship beyond isolation and alienation. To imagine initiation as public and necessary, and reconciliation as private and optional, is illusion at its most dangerous. It is like inviting someone to become half a person. Yet there continues to exist an anthropological double standard in our sacramental celebrations.

For initiation, the working anthropology tends to be communal and process centered; for reconciliation, it is privatized and event centered. As a result, initiation celebrates conversion into community, invites the ministry of the whole community and respects the faith journey of each person. In contrast, reconciliation "celebrates" conversion as a one-on-one experience between penitent and God, restricts ministerial roles to the ordained and wraps the entire sacramental experience into a single event.

Fundamental to the continued implementation of the *Rite of Christian Initiation of Adults* is the rediscovery of this inherent connection between initiation and reconciliation. We are challenged to carry our working anthropology beyond the baptismal font to the reconciliation room and far, far beyond. Celebrations of reconciliation throughout the initiation journey will confirm and effect the divine activity of a loving God to conquer isolation and alienation and fulfill every human longing. The graced moment of fulfillment, when the story of Jesus is connected with the story of the community and is connected with the story of each member of the community, must not go uncelebrated. Our pastoral challenge is to connect these moments with ritual expressions of conversion into, commitment to and celebration in community.[11] In this way, we begin a recovery process that will reestablish trust in the powerful efficacy of the rites of "second baptism."

THE CHALLENGE FOR US

In the first part of this chapter, I offered an unfamiliar answer to the pastoral question posed by baptized Christians who present themselves for full initiation into the Catholic community: Reconcile them. It was the answer Stephen understood as entirely sufficient in his disagreement with the more conservative pastoral practice of the North African church. Reconciliation was the second baptism that admitted those previously baptized into another communion to the eucharistic table of the Roman Catholic Church.

As we struggle to become both initiating and reconciling communities of faith, Stephen's answer still challenges us today.[12] True reconciling communities, faced with the pastoral opportunity of already baptized Christians presenting themselves for full initiation, clearly comprehend that a "one-size-fits-all" catechumenate just does not work. Reconciling communities embrace the hard work of discernment that both stretches and strengthens all pastoral and catechetical wisdom. What must be the focus of the journey for these Advent souls, the "already but not yet"? Will theirs be essentially a journey of reconciliation integrated with adapted rites of initiation, or will the focus be on initiation and awakening faith, with adapted rites of reconciliation? Only those privileged to walk with them as they make the journey will be in a position to discern these matters. While at first it may seem to be unknown territory, the spirit of Christ active in the community will transform the journey and those who make it into holy ground.

ENDNOTES

1. See *Code of Canon Law,* canon 869, and *Rite of Christian Initiation of Adults,* appendix III, National Statutes on the Catechumenate, #37 (U.S. only).

2. Obviously, in instances where the baptized person is genuinely uncatechized, certain rites of the order of Christian initiation of adults are appropriate (cf. #401–402 U.S.; 377–378 Can.; National Statutes on the Catechumenate, #31, U.S. only). The documents make it patently clear, however, that the status of baptized Christians differs from that of catechumens.

3. This is perfectly in accord with the instruction given in the *Rite of Christian Initiation of Adults,* #408 U.S., 384 Can.

4. Much fruitful work was done by the cultural anthropologist Mary Douglas on the correlation between a community's trust in the efficacy of its rituals and the degree (high or low) of its internal organization. See especially *Natural Symbols* (New York: Pantheon Books, 1982), 1–18.

5. See James Dallen and Joseph Favazza, *Removing the Barriers: The Practice of Reconciliation* (Chicago: Liturgy Training Publications, 1991), 21–22; and James Dallen, *The Reconciling Community* (New York: Pueblo Publishing Co., 1986), 374–385.

6. The North American Forum on the Catechumenate, Falls Church, Virginia, offers an institute titled "ReMembering Church," which presents a model for reconciling alienated Catholics through a process-centered ritual.

7. For this historical treatment, I admit my indebtedness to the recent article by J. P. Burns, "On Rebaptism: Social Organization in the Third Century Church," *Journal of Early Christian Studies* (winter 1993): 367–403. For a more complete explanation of the penitential practice of the North African Church, see my own work, *The Order of Penitents: Historical Roots and Pastoral Future* (Collegeville: Liturgical Press, 1988), 202–230.

8. The pertinent letters from Novatian and the Roman church are found as Epp. 30, 31 and 36 in G. W. Clark, *The Letters of St. Cyprian, Ancient Christian Writers*, vols. 43, 45, 46, 47 (New York: Newman Press, 1984–1989).

9. In the *Rite of Christian Initiation of Adults*, National Statute #28 (U.S. only) refers to priests who have the faculty to confirm "a baptized Catholic who has been an apostate from the faith." This is a specific canonical situation, which is separate from the issue at stake here. Again, the third-century issue of rebaptism is used here to highlight only the pastoral situation of those first baptized into another Christian community and not the canonical situation of those who have explicitly rejected their initiation and formation as Catholic.

10. The issue of rebaptism is discussed in Epp. 69–75 of Cyprian's letters. However, the specific disagreement is discussed most explicitly in Epp. 74 and 75.

11. See Dallen and Favazza, *Removing the Barriers*, 41–63.

12. See Ibid., 65–76.

CHAPTER FOUR

The Effects of Baptism

MARK SEARLE

All-powerful and ever-living God,
be present to these mysteries of your love,
be present to these sacraments.
Send the spirit of adoption
to refashion the multitudes
to be born to you from the font of baptism,
so that what is performed by our lowly ministry
may be rendered effectual by your power.

(Translation of the prayer after the reading from Ezekiel 36
for the Easter Vigil, from the Missale Romanum)

Consider two rather familiar scenarios:

A catechist who has worked closely with a group of catechumens and has witnessed their faith and the transformation wrought in them by the Spirit now has to talk to them about baptism. What can he or she say? How can he or she tell them they will become children of God, or will receive the Holy Spirit, or will have their sins forgiven? Have they not received these graces already? Are they not already members of the church? What does baptism add?

Candidates for full communion remain in their places while their unbaptized companions step forward for the rite of election, for the scrutinies and for baptism. Why? Because they happened to be baptized as infants, although they did not grow up as Christians. Are they not being barred from the best part of the whole process by a technicality?

In these ways, the hoary old problems of sacramental theology—how do sacraments confer grace and what has that to do with their signification—continue to surface in pastoral practice. One temptation too easily succumbed to today is to sidestep the issue by speaking of the sacraments as "celebrations." This emphasizes what the sacraments *signify* but avoids the issue of whether they actually make a difference. One then can think of marriage as a celebration of love, or baptism as a celebration of faith (or worse, welcome), in much the same way that one celebrates graduation with a party—a way of marking something that already has happened. Unfortunately, this solution is no solution: It neither resolves the kind of practical difficulties illustrated by the second case above nor does justice to the Christian tradition that sacramental celebrations make a difference—they *confer* what they signify.

In this chapter we will reexamine this issue in the hope of finding a more satisfying approach to the problem. It will not be possible to deal explicitly with all aspects of the problem, but the approach suggested will have to be one that also allows for a satisfactory solution to related problems, such as that of how to reconcile the church's confidence in the efficacy of the sacraments with the need to safeguard God's sovereign freedom. We can't be satisfied with an explanation of the sacraments that domesticates God to being one who turns on the spigot of grace whenever the appropriate words are said. On the other hand, we also need an explanation of how the sacraments work that stays close to the actual rites we use instead of developing entirely in abstraction from them, as once was the case and often still is.

THE RICH SYMBOL

The church praises God in the blessing of baptismal water at the Easter Vigil with the words: "you have made [water] a rich symbol of the *grace* you give us in this sacrament." That grace is identified in the same prayer with a number of images: It is "an end to sin and a new beginning of goodness." It is liberation and cleansing from sin. It is burial with Christ in sacramental death in the hope of rising with him to "newness of life." Earlier in the Vigil the readings and prayers speak of baptism as "the increase of your chosen people," "the new creation" and so on. More images can be found in the *Exsultet*, in the rites following baptism and in the liturgies of the Easter season.

In attempting to evaluate these splendid claims, the first thing that must be done is to sort them into different categories in terms of the relationships they represent. After all, some of these images represent a new relationship with God, others a new relationship with Christ, and still others a new relationship to the church as people of God.

These texts do not speak of a new relationship to the Spirit, though the Spirit figures rather prominently, especially in the blessing of the font. The liturgy tends, rather, to take up the Johannine image of the efficacy of baptism being attributable both to the water and to the Spirit. On the basis of the blessing of the font and of the prayer cited at the beginning of this chapter (which used to lead into it in the old rite), I am inclined to think that "water" and "Spirit" correspond to "our lowly ministry" on the one hand and to "your [God's] power" on the other. "Water" is metonymy for the baptismal liturgy as a whole and the water rite in particular. These constitute the "signifier" or "outward sign," whereas the "Spirit" is a similar metonym of the divine presence and action signified by the gathered church and its ritual action. These two dimensions of the sign are what "cause" the effects of baptism mentioned above: the new relationship with the church, the new relationship with Christ and the new relationship with God. We must explore each of these in turn, and we can do so by recalling that, in Catholic sacramental theology, the effects of the sacrament are twofold: It confers a "character" and it gives grace.

SACRAMENTAL CHARACTER

The doctrine of sacramental character, which originated in an attempt to explain why baptism could not be repeated, has undergone considerable evolution and some quite unnecessary obfuscation over the centuries. In particular, attempts to explain it as a "mark on the soul" constitute a quite needless reification of what is less an ontological reality than a social reality.

"Character," I believe, is best understood as the irrevocable benefit of membership with the church, accruing to all who are validly baptized. This is no different from the practice of "naturalizing" aliens, in which as a result of a properly conducted ceremony non-Americans are granted American citizenship. Just as baptized Christians are not eligible for baptism, so American citizens are not eligible for naturalization. One could imagine that someone born overseas of American parents and raised in some less happy clime might well feel, on returning to this country, that he or she would like to swear allegiance to the flag in front of a judge and so become a citizen all over again; but there is no such convention, so it cannot be done. Similarly, the church decided centuries ago that persons once baptized always would remain members of the church, even if they "lapsed." The irreversibility of membership in the church is what "character" denotes.

With that irreversible gift of membership, as with U.S. citizenship, came certain inalienable privileges and responsibilities. The difference, of course, is that the church claims to be a very different kind of society, and membership in it is understood as giving rise to very different kinds of rights and duties. In particular, the church claims to be the people of God and the body of Christ on earth, the sacrament of his abiding presence and activity in the world. That presence and activity is mediated by the Holy Spirit, who is the soul of the church and its bond of unity. This means that someone who undergoes the sacraments of initiation into the church is *ipso facto* claimed for God (this organization is, after all, the people of God) and assimilated to Christ (this organization exists to be the sacrament or sign of Christ's presence and work in the world). So we have to say that simply by virtue of a valid celebration of the sacrament, a person is irreversibly claimed for God and irreversibly invested with the responsibility of being part of the sign that the church is meant to be.

The church is a sign of Christ as mediator between God and the human race. Christ as mediator is both the spokesman for his fellow human beings before God and the bringer of God's gifts into this world. That double mission now is exercised in and through the church, and all baptized persons are deputed to share that mediatorial, or priestly, function of Christ in virtue of their membership in the community of the baptized. That is why Thomas Aquinas describes "character" not in terms of a mark on the soul but in functional terms, as a certain participation in the priesthood of Christ to be exercised in accordance with one's position in the church.

The traditional teaching of the church is that this "character" is conferred *ex opere operato*, i.e., in virtue of the ceremonies being carried out correctly and with the appropriate intention. There is nothing magical about this. American citizenship is conferred *ex opere operato*; couples who fulfill all the legal requirements for marriage are married *ex opere operato*; and someone who enlists in the army becomes *ex opere operato* a soldier. Note that this does not of itself enable the immigrant to speak English, ensure that the couple really love each other or guarantee the new soldier's competence or even loyalty. But in each case, certain rights and responsibilities come with the new role. "Character" is this new role.

The act of investing a person with such a role is obviously best done in public so that the person's new identity is immediately recognized and sustained. Without such social support given in one way or another, the newly baptized persons, like newly wed couples or newly naturalized citizens, risk finding their sense of identity quickly eroding. That is why the church prefers public baptism and solemn ritual. Above all, it is in the liturgy of Easter night that the new identity of the baptized as members of this community, assuming these responsibilities, is dramatically clear:

1) They side with the church in judging Satan's promises to be "empty" and in renouncing him. Conversely, they also side with the church in giving over their lives to God "the Father almighty" and to the Christ whom the church calls "our Lord." They join the church in adopting the church's position in the world.

2) The water rite clearly involves the disowning of one's old identity and the assumption of a new identity when it is an act of washing. When it is an act of immersion, it also assimilates the candidates to Jesus in his own baptism by John and in his death and burial. This—as opposed to saluting the flag or signing one's name—clearly indicates that membership in the church is membership in the social body that is the sign and sacrament of his presence in the world; the baptized are invested with the responsibility of becoming credible icons of Christ just as the soldier is invested with the responsibility of defending her or his country.

3) The postbaptismal anointing, with its formula, "As Christ was anointed prophet, priest and king, so may you live always as members of his body," and the investiture of the neophytes with white garments and burning candles all speak eloquently of the new role assumed by those who are baptized.

Note that these are new roles. Though catechumens are members of the church, they are so as catechumens, not as full-fledged members enjoying all the privileges and responsibilities of the baptized. They are related to the baptized as novices are related to the professed in religious communities. And note that these new roles and responsibilities are assigned *ex opere operato,* by virtue, simply, of the fact of baptism.

THE GRACE OF THE SACRAMENT

After baptism we can be absolutely sure that the former catechumens are now baptized Christians who belong to God; they have the responsibility to witness to Christ and can never be baptized again. They have the corresponding right to full participation in the sacramental life of the church in accordance with church law. Of this we can be sure, because baptism, whatever else it may be, is a conventional ceremony that has certain conventional effects that are derived from the nature of the community and are enshrined in church law.

The other effect attributed by theologians to baptism—sanctifying grace or a living relationship with God—is a different matter altogether. Having a legal relationship to the church is not the same as having a personal relationship with God. The personal relationship, as opposed to the merely formal one of being a member of God's people, cannot be established ritually or *ex opere operato*. Like all relationships, it takes time and a measure of openness on the part of the recipient to develop. In that sense it is misleading to say that, in baptism, sanctifying grace is conferred *ex opere operato;* it would be more precise to say that God *offers* a personal and social relationship in baptism because the initiative is always from the side of God, as the term "grace" implies. But for there to be a real relationship, that offer has to be accepted. To become God's temples, sharers in the divine life, Christians must at least be as open to God as their age and personality allow. God will not force people against their will. Just as marriage is no guarantee of love, or citizenship a guarantee of loyalty, so baptism is no guarantee of being in a state of grace.

Nonetheless, the offer of grace is there, for that is what is signified not only by the sacramental rite but by the sacramental church that celebrates it. In the words of Vatican II, from the *Constitution on the Sacred Liturgy (Sacrosanctum concilium)*, 2:

> It is of the essence of the church that she be both human
> and divine, visible and yet invisibly endowed, eager to act
> and yet devoted to contemplation, present in this world

and yet not at home in it. She is all these things in such a way that in her, the human is directed and subordinated to the divine, the visible likewise to the invisible, action to contemplation, and this present world to that city yet to come which we seek.

If it is of the essence of the church to be both human and divine, to be both an empirical reality and a communion of life hidden with God in Christ, nowhere is this double dimension more explicitly acknowledged than in the liturgy. Here the assembly and its rituals constitute the human sign of the invisible, divine realities in which Christians become engaged through a contemplative action, an active contemplation, doing what Christians do in faith and prayer.

From this follows a double corollary. First, the nature of the church as sign and the nature of its liturgical activity as sacramental mean that the presumption always will be that the offer of grace is made and accepted in the sacraments. It may well happen that the sinner seeking absolution is not repentant or that the candidate for baptism is merely going through the motions, just as it may happen that a couple might marry one another for reasons that have little or nothing to do with mutual love. But such cases always must be exceptional and the church has the responsibility of ensuring that only those whose hearts are open to the love of God come to the sacraments. Thus we always will assume, unless and until we have reason to believe otherwise, that the sacrament is not only valid and confers its *character* but that it is fruitful in mediating a living relationship between the candidates and God in Christ. It is on such an assumption that the church presumes to celebrate the eucharist for the newly baptized and to speak of them as new creations, adopted children of God, living members of Christ and temples of the Holy Spirit.

However, the church also recognizes that if her assemblies and their rites are truly signs of God's gracious love toward the people of God, it is entirely due to God's free initiative and in no way something that the church can conjure up. This, too, is given strong expression in the baptismal liturgy in the blessing of the font. If grace were given by virtue of the rite alone, there would be no need to recall God's saving acts in the past or Christ's mandate to the church to go and baptize. Above all, there would be no need to pray over and over that God would bless the water (read: "water rites") by sending the Holy Spirit. The point of such prayer, surely, is that unless the action of the Christian is accompanied by God's own action, the rites will remain hollow signs and empty symbols.

Such is the quandary of the church. The rites signify something that the church cannot guarantee: the gift of the Spirit. Baptism is effective only in terms of the relationship of the Christian with God if it is baptism both by water (the liturgy) and by the Spirit (the divine presence and action that signifies). Ideally, every baptism is fully effective, not merely making people members of the church and assimilating them formally to Christ but also engaging them in the very life of God in Christ. But because those two things are quite distinct effects— one relating persons socially to the church and the other relating persons to God—it is necessary to insist that the social effects of baptism may be realized through a valid performance of the rite, even if the offer of grace is not taken up. However much they *ought* to go together, it is necessary both pastorally and theologically to recognize that they can be separated.

On the other hand, not only does the social effect of baptism (character) imply participation in the divine life through the Spirit of Christ, but its responsibilities cannot be carried out without that life of grace. The individual, like the community and like the sacramental rite, is an empty sign if he or she is not in fact living the Christian life out of the depths of the Spirit. Thus the truthfulness of the sacramental sign is always in jeopardy—in the liturgy, in the life of the church and in the life of the individual—when the human person is not in fact directed and subordinated to the divine, the visible to the invisible, action to contemplation and this world to the city yet to come.

For this reason, "it is necessary that the faithful come to [the liturgy] with proper dispositions, that their thoughts match their words, and that they cooperate with divine grace lest they receive it in vain" (see again the words of the anointing after baptism). This in turn means adequate spiritual preparation for the celebration on the part of all participants and a style of celebration that bespeaks the awesome mysteries signified by what we do. Most of all, it means realizing that Christians do not just perform or receive sacraments: Christians are themselves constitutive of the sacramental sign. Its credibility depends not just on valid matter and form but on the openness of all the participants to the divine life that seeks an epiphany in them.

The fact that God has initiated this relationship long before the catechumens get near the font, just as God's merciful forgiveness reaches out to people long before they get to the confessional, does not make the ritual redundant, however. Rather, with the public ritual the personal relationship with God takes on a new form and enters upon a new stage. It is there that people fully assume responsibility for what God is doing in their lives and allow that action to find the social and historical form that God's redemption of humanity requires. If it were only one's inner life with God that counted, sacraments would be nothing more than private "means of grace," supports for an ongoing interior life. But just as character implies grace, so grace implies character. In other words, a person's relationship to God is always in Christ and in the church, and it seeks expression in the social role identified with *character:* an ecclesial vocation to participate in Christ's work of mediating between God and humanity, in publicly acknowledging the name of God in worship and in bringing the gifts of God to the world for which they are destined.

Thus the real issue in the sacraments is not what the sacraments do as *things* but what sacramental people are doing together — what God is able to do through the people of God working together to realize God's rule on earth.

CHAPTER FIVE

Normative Dimensions of Initiation

RONALD A. OAKHAM

I n Chapter 3, "Reconciliation as Second Baptism," Joseph Favazza mentions "a widespread pastoral amnesia" regarding the relationship between initiation and reconciliation. It is my experience that this same pastoral amnesia also exists in regard to the norms for Christian initiation when the initiation of an adult doesn't require all the various steps and periods of the catechumenate process. Too often in these cases the pastoral minister reverts to pre–Vatican II forms (private instruction and private ritual, albeit using the current rites), ignoring the norms established for initiation by the promulgation of this order of Christian initiation.

The *Rite of Christian Initiation of Adults* is an ordering of rites for adult initiation—in all circumstances. Part I of the text details the full-scale catechumenal process, not as the only path to the eucharistic table but as the basic path, the norm for Christian initiation. Part II lists alternative paths to be taken in response to particular circumstances (e.g., children of catechetical age; people in danger of death; baptized, uncatechized Christians; baptized, catechized Christians). Each of these alternatives relies on some normative features set down in part I.

In this chapter I will identify these normative features as they appear in the basic pattern for initiation of unbaptized adults, and, at times, make brief comments about their application to the baptized

Christian's situation. In the second part of this book, "Pastoral Implementation," I will refer back to these norms and draw more explicit implications for the adaptations required for initiating baptized Christians.

THE NORM OF BAPTISM

Before I examine the various normative dimensions of the catechumenate, a brief exploration of the norm of baptism and the notion of norm as it is used here is needed. As Aidan Kavanagh notes,

> [The *Rite of Christian Initiation of Adults*] purpose is less to give liturgical recipes than to shift the church's initiatory polity from one conventional norm centering on infant baptism to the more traditional norm centering on adults. Nowhere does the document say this in so many words. If this is not the case, however, then the document not only makes no sense but is vain and fatuous. Its extensive and sensitive dispositions for gradually incorporating adult converts into communities of faith nowhere suggest that this process should be regarded as the rare exception. On the contrary, from deep within the Roman tradition it speaks of the process presumptively as normative. [1]

Kavanagh goes on to explore the norm of eucharist,[2] as defined by the Second Vatican Council, as an example of what he is writing regarding baptism. He then explicates the norm of baptism:

> The norm of baptism was stated by the Council in a more diffused form than that of the eucharist, but no less definitely, to be solemn sacramental initiation done especially at the paschal vigil and preceded by a catechumenate of serious content and considerable duration.[3]

In the midst of this section, Kavanagh explains the meaning of the term "norm" as it is being used here:

A *norm* in this sense has nothing to do with the number of times a thing is done, but it has everything to do with the standard according to which a thing is done. So long as the norm is in place both in practice and in the awareness of those who are engaged in it, the situation is capable of being judged "normal" even though the norm must be departed from to some extent, even frequently, due to exigencies of time, place, pastoral considerations, physical inabilities, or whatever. Yet to the extent possible, the norm must always be achieved to some extent lest it slip imperceptibly into the status of a mere "ideal" all wish for but are under no obligation to realize.[4]

Thus if the *Rite of Christian Initiation of Adults* is the norm for all initiation, then not only does the initiation of any adult (which includes children of catechetical age) in whatever circumstance come under its influence, but the baptism of infants does, too. Consequently, even if a parish never has the opportunity to initiate an unbaptized adult, it must be familiar with the full catechumenal process and the norms it expresses so that the parish may shape all of its initiatory practices according to the church's established norm.

NORMATIVE DIMENSIONS

From my study of and work with the *Rite of Christian Initiation of Adults,* I have identified seven areas of concern in which the document sets forth norms:

1) The overall character of the experience
2) The full use of symbols
3) The context in which initiation occurs
4) The catechetical formation provided
5) The way in which rituals are celebrated
6) The time of initiation
7) The integrity of sacramental sequence

From the very beginning of the *praenotanda* (introductory paragraphs), the document explicates the character expected of initiation:

> The whole initiation must bear a markedly paschal charac-
> ter, since the initiation of Christians is the first sacramen-
> tal sharing in Christ's dying and rising. (#8)

This "paschal character" is most often spoken of throughout the ritual text with the term *conversion.* Consequently, the initiation process
is primarily concerned with fostering a conversion experience that is
being prompted by the Lord ("their hearts being opened by the Spirit,"
#36). The rite is also clear about to what this conversion is directed:
"to the Lord" (#36). To emphasize further that this conversion is to
the Lord and not to Catholicism (as common references would lead
us to believe), the National Statutes for the implementation of the
initiation process in the United States note that

> The term "convert" should be reserved strictly for those
> converted from unbelief to Christian belief and never used
> of those baptized Christians who are received into the full
> communion of the Catholic church. (National Statutes,
> #2, U.S. only)

The document takes the stance that someone who wishes to be
initiated into the Catholic church does so because God is prompting
within that person something that manifests itself as an experience of
being "called away from sin and drawn into the mystery of God's love"
(#37). This conversion to the Lord will look different for each person, but whether we are focusing on someone who is coming to an initial belief in Jesus or on someone who is a highly committed Christian,
the dynamics are the same: dying and rising. The rite is clear: All initiation must bear a paschal character.

Thus even when we are dealing with a baptized, catechized adult
who is coming to us from a mainline Protestant church (e.g., Lutheran,
Methodist), the initiation process must first and foremost seek to foster the conversion going on within the person's life. For the initiation

minister to treat it as merely a change of confession (e.g., from Presbyterianism to Catholicism) is to undercut God's activity. The task of the initiation minister is not just to educate the candidate about Catholicism but to discern, along with the candidate, what it is that God is prompting in his or her life. What is God's Spirit inspiring him or her "to die to" so that he or she may "rise to new life"? Once this is discerned, then the ministers will be able to call forth from the church the people, the teachings and the traditions that will foster this conversion. The Christian community will be able to provide what is needed to accompany the candidate on the paschal journey into a deeper relationship with Christ in the Catholic church.

The Full Use of Symbols

As a part of the restoration and renewal of the church's sacramental rites, Vatican II called for a greater use of the various symbols used in our rituals. It put into effect a deliberate effort to move away from the minimalist approach to symbols that had become standard. The spirit of this move is seen in various conciliar and postconciliar documents.

Addressing the celebration of the eucharist, *The Constitution on the Sacred Liturgy (Sacrosanctum concilium)*, 55, states:

> The more perfect form of participation in the Mass whereby the faithful, after the priest's communion, receive the Lord's Body from the same sacrifice, is warmly recommended.[5]

The *General Instruction of the Roman Missal* (240) expands on the council's initial statement:

> Holy communion has a more complete form as a sign when it is received under both kinds. For in this manner of reception a fuller light shines on the sign of the eucharistic banquet. Moreover there is a clearer expression of that will by which the new and everlasting covenant is ratified in the blood of the Lord and of the relationship of the

eucharistic banquet to the eschatological banquet in the Father's kingdom.[6]

The *Rite of Christian Initiation of Adults* presumes that this "more complete form" will be used for baptism and during the neophytes' first sharing in the celebration of the eucharist:

> In the celebration of baptism the washing with water should take on its full importance as the sign of that mystical sharing in Christ's death and resurrection through which those who believe in his name die to sin and rise to eternal life. Either immersion or the pouring of water should be chosen for the rite, whichever will serve in individual cases and in the various traditions and circumstances to ensure the clear understanding that this washing is not a mere purification rite but the sacrament of being joined to Christ. (#213 U.S., #206 Can.)

> When in communion they receive the body that was given for us and the blood that was shed, the neophytes are strengthened in the gifts they have already received and are given a foretaste of the eternal banquet. (#217 U.S., #210 Can.)

In its *National Statutes,* the U.S. edition includes a stronger statement building upon the international text's somewhat egalitarian approach to immersion or the pouring of water for baptism.

> Baptism by immersion is the fuller and more expressive sign of the sacrament and, therefore, is preferred. Although it is not yet a common practice in the United States, provision should be made for its more frequent use in the baptism of adults. At the least, the provision of the *Rite of Christian Initiation of Adults* for partial immersion, namely, immersion of the candidate's head, should be taken into account. (National Statutes, #17 U.S. only)

We can see from these statements that the use of the fuller forms of symbols is normative for the sacramental life of the church.

Unfortunately, even when the catechumenate is the appropriate path for a particular person, there is often a tendency toward minimalism (especially on the part of the presiders). For example, in the Rite of Acceptance into the Order of Catechumens, the choice of signing either the forehead alone or the forehead and other parts of the body is given. Many presiders (or other ministers) decide to use the lesser symbol, signing the forehead only. Where such an attitude prevails, one can expect the same approach to the initiation of the baptized Christian. But even when the parish's practice is to use fuller symbols with the unbaptized, one can find a latent, if not blatant, tendency for minimalism with the baptized candidate.

The *Rite of Christian Initiation of Adults* is clear: The norm for all initiation rites is to use the fuller and more complete form of any and all symbols.

THE CONTEXT IN WHICH INITIATION OCCURS

The norm concerning the context of initiation that is promulgated within the ritual text has its roots in a number of Vatican II documents, three of which are particularly important for our purposes.

In the *Decree on the Church's Missionary Activity (Ad gentes)*, 14, the Council declared:

> This Christian initiation, which takes place during the catechumenate, should not be left entirely to the priests and catechists, but should be the concern of the whole Christian community, especially of the sponsors, so that from the beginning the catechumens will feel that they belong to the people of God.[7]

In the *Decree on the Ministry and Life of Priests (Presbyterorum ordinis)*, 6, we read:

> A local community ought not merely to promote the care of the faithful within itself, but should be imbued with the missionary spirit and smooth the path to Christ for all people. But it must regard as its special charge those under

instruction and the newly converted who are gradually educated in knowing and living the Christian life.[8]

Although it is addressing liturgical celebrations in general, *The Constitution on the Sacred Liturgy (Sacrosanctum concilium)*, 27, can easily and rightly be understood to refer to our initiation rites when it states:

> It must be emphasized that rites which are meant to be celebrated in common, with the faithful present and actively participating, should as far as possible be celebrated in that way rather than by an individual and quasi-privately.[9]

These council statements lay the foundation for the order of Christian initiation's statement in its *praenotanda:*

> The people of God, as represented by the local church, should understand and show by their concern that the initiation of adults is the responsibility of all the baptized. (#9)

Throughout the text, reference is made to the active presence of the community both in the catechetical formation and in the liturgical celebrations. With the promulgation of this ritual text, the previous practice of private instruction and private rites has been abrogated. Consequently, even for the well-catechized Christian, whose journey to the eucharistic table will be shorter and simpler than that of the unbaptized adult, the communal nature of the initiation process must be recognizable. The Christian community is the context within which initiation happens. The community's presence and active participation in whatever formation is provided, as well as in the rituals celebrated, is a part of the symbolic structure of the initiation sacraments. Thus the parish must strive to use as full a form of this symbol as possible.

THE CATECHETICAL FORMATION PROVIDED

Paragraph 75 of the ritual text, the "charter" of pastoral formation and guidance during the catechumenate, is built upon a statement from *The Decree on the Church's Missionary Activity (Ad gentes),* 14:

> The catechumenate is not a mere expounding of dogmatic
> truths and norms of morality, but a period of formation
> in the whole Christian life, an apprenticeship of sufficient
> duration.[10]

The church envisions an apprenticeship, not a prep school. The catechumenate is a time of being mentored into a way of life, not a time for disengaged, theoretical ruminating about theological concepts and moral principles. The intent of the rite is not merely theological education or preparation for the sacramental rites of initiation. Rather, the rite seeks to set forth a guide for developing a process that will prepare those who enter into it for living a radically vibrant Christian life.

To this end, then, the question that needs to be explored (though not explicitly) in the beginning phases of an individual's initiation is, What is needed to enable this person to enter into full, conscious and active participation in the life of the Catholic community? The focus must be on the individual's need, not on the parish's program. What the parish will provide is reflective of and responsive to these needs.

Paragraph 78 of the ritual text states the norm for catechetical formation quite succinctly:

> The instruction that the catechumens receive during this
> period should be of a kind that while presenting Catholic
> teaching in its entirety also enlightens faith, directs the
> heart toward God, fosters participation in the liturgy,
> inspires apostolic activity, and nurtures a life completely
> in accord with the spirit of Christ.

In other words, the rite envisions that the norm for catechetical formation is an apprenticeship.

THE WAY IN WHICH RITUALS ARE CELEBRATED

In addition to the use of fuller forms of the symbols and the carrying out of ritual celebrations in such a manner that they demonstrate that initiation is the work of the whole church, the rite contains another norm for these celebrations. The various rites are to be celebrated at different times within the initiation journey and not in a compressed manner, such as is usually experienced with the baptism of infants. This is because these rites act as "steps marking the catechumen's progress, as they pass, so to speak, through another doorway or ascend to the next level" (#6).

THE TIME OF INITIATION

The rituals of initiation need to be located within the personal and communal history of those involved. The ritual text repeatedly makes such references as "at the right time" and "not too early." Only when the person's own journey corresponds to that which the rite celebrates should there be a celebration. But the right time is not determined only by the readiness of the individual; it also depends on the readiness of the community that is doing the initiating. When can the community accommodate itself to this ritual action? When does the church's own rhythm of celebrating the complete mystery of Christ's redeeming action lend itself to incorporating ritual actions of initiation?

Including the question of the community's readiness in deciding when to celebrate is not unheard of in our society. In preparing for a wedding, the bride and groom do not base the date of their celebration only on their readiness to declare their consent to marry; they also consider when their relatives and friends can join in the celebration. Where these two dimensions of their lives best coincide is where the date is set; and if it means waiting a few months, they wait.

For the rituals of election, scrutinies and the Easter sacraments, the ritual text is very clear about when the rites should be celebrated: during the paschal cycle (Lent-Triduum-Eastertime).

> The period of purification and enlightenment ordinarily coincides with Lent and the period of postbaptismal catechesis or mystagogy with the Easter season. All the resources of Lent should be brought to bear as a more intense preparation of the elect and the Easter Vigil should be regarded as the proper time for the sacraments of initiation. (#8)

The rite does allow for exceptions (see #26–30), but it approaches these precisely as exceptions and thus not as frequent experiences. And, it still locates sacramental initiation on a Sunday, the church's weekly Easter.

The ritual text isn't as definitive about the appropriate time for the rite of acceptance, but once one studies the particular rite itself, it becomes clearer. Appropriate communal times are when the church's liturgy focuses on taking up the cross and following Jesus, on Jesus' invitation to the various people he meets to come and follow, or on a disciple's proclamation of faith in the Lord Jesus as the messiah, the one who is to come.

Individual and communal readiness constitute the norm for the time of initiation.

THE INTEGRITY OF SACRAMENTAL SEQUENCE

Both the ritual text for Christian initiation and canon law establish the traditional sequence and continuous celebration of baptism, confirmation and eucharist as the norm (see #206, 215 U.S.; #198, 208 Can.; canons 886, 883 §2, 885 §2). Because this sequence has not been the general experience in the United States, the National Statutes in the U.S. edition of the *Rite of Christian Initiation of Adults* make a great effort to underline this norm. Thirteen of thirty-seven paragraphs address this issue in one way or another. Two paragraphs are particularly strong on this point.

> In order to signify clearly the interrelation or coalescence of the three sacraments which are required for full Christian initiation (canon 842 §2), adult candidates, including children of catechetical age, are to receive baptism, confirmation and eucharist in a single eucharistic celebration, whether at the Easter Vigil or, if necessary, at some other time. (National Statutes, #14, U.S. only)

> Since those who have the faculty to confirm are bound to exercise it in accord with canon 885 §2 and may not be

> prohibited from using the faculty, a diocesan bishop who
> is desirous of confirming neophytes should reserve to him-
> self the baptism of adults in accord with canon 863.
> (National Statutes, #13, U.S. only)

Because of the twentieth-century custom in North America that
inverts the sequence of baptism, confirmation and eucharist (to baptism, eucharist and confirmation), this norm is often overlooked. This
is especially true if the bishop is coming during the Easter season to
celebrate confirmation with children. Too often in such cases, pastors
decide to delay confirming both those being baptized and those being
received. Other times this norm is ignored because the pastor is just
not aware of the changes regarding the faculty to confirm (this will be
addressed briefly in chapter 9). Whatever the reasons are for ignoring
this norm, doing so distorts the church's understanding of full initiation: Confirmation then becomes the fullness of initiation, not the
eucharist.[11] Initiation ministers need to take seriously the church's
attempt to restore the initiation sacraments to their ancient sequence.
Adhering to the norm will foster this restoration work.

CONCLUSION

To be sure, this chapter is not an exhaustive treatise on the norms for
initiation established by the *Rite of Christian Initiation of Adults*. It does
enumerate, however, the norms that I continually observe being ignored
in one way or another as parishes continue to implement the church's
revised approach to the initiation of adults. If the ongoing restoration of the catechumenate as the church's policy for initiation is to be
faithful to the vision brought to birth at the Second Vatican Council,
we must be aware of these norms and must scrutinize our pastoral
practice to see that they are being incorporated as fully as possible.

ENDNOTES

1. Aidan Kavanagh, *The Shape of Baptism: The Rite of Christian Initiation* (New York: Pueblo Publishing Co., 1978), 106.

2. Ibid., 106–108. Or see endnote 21 of chapter 2 of this book.

3. Ibid., 109.

4. Ibid., 108.

5. Austin Flannery, ed., *Vatican Council ii: The Conciliar and Post Conciliar Documents* (Northport, New York: Costello Publishing Company, 1975), 18.

6. Elizabeth Hoffman, ed. *The Liturgy Documents: A Parish Resource* (Chicago: Liturgy Training Publications, 1985), 84.

7. Flannery, ibid., 828.

8. Ibid., 874.

9. Ibid., 11.

10. Ibid., 828.

11. In addition to Rita Ferrone's treatment of the church's understanding of communion in chapter 2 of this book, see Nathan Mitchell, *Eucharist as Sacrament of Initiation* (Chicago: Liturgy Training Publications, 1994).

PART II

Pastoral Implementation

CHAPTER SIX

Formation of Uncatechized Christians

RONALD A. OAKHAM

Even though uncatechized adults have not yet heard the message of the mystery of Christ, their status differs from that of catechumens, since by baptism they have already become members of the church and children of God. Hence their conversion is based on the baptism they have already received, the effects of which they must develop.   **(#400 U.S., 376 Can.)**

The first clue that something was wrong came during the fourth week of Lent one year. We had just celebrated the second scrutiny (adapted to include the baptized candidates), the reflection session following the celebration had ended, and the catechumenate group was lingering for some social time with their godparents/sponsors, family and team members. Mark, a baptized, uncatechized Christian, was sharing with me his very positive reactions to all the ritual components of his initiation. He concluded his comments with what I found to be an unnerving statement: "It all leaves me wishing I hadn't already been baptized; then I could be baptized at the Easter Vigil."

Like neon blazing in the night, our failure flashed before me. In working to help Mark develop his faith life as a Catholic Christian, we unconsciously had diminished his respect for his baptism. We had undermined this sacred reality in his life. I realized then that at our next team meeting, we had to talk.

I wish I could say this was an isolated event, but through the years I have heard other leaders tell similar stories when I share this one. The stories cry out to me that there is something very wrong in many catechumenates. Even with our great esteem for baptism, we are not fostering a respect for it within the lives of those who come to us already baptized. Yet the rite is clear that this is the starting point of their formation: "their conversion is based on the baptism they have already received, the effects of which they must develop" (#400 U.S., 376 Can.). Of all the issues surrounding the question of what should be provided in the pastoral formation for baptized, uncatechized Christians, how to foster a respect for their baptism is the one about which I have heard the least discussion and seen the least written. Therefore, before addressing the issue of formation in general, I want to spend some time considering this particular aspect as a part of the overall formation.

QUESTION: FOSTERING RESPECT FOR BAPTISM

When I asked catechumenate directors around the country about what they did to help baptized Christians develop a respect for their baptism, I was saddened by the dearth of responses. Beyond recognizing the validity of their baptism, using the adapted rites and being clear about who is a catechumen and who is a candidate, most weren't doing much more. But some were.

PASTORAL RESPONSES

The parish I found addressing the question of baptized candidates the most is St. Philip in Bakersfield, California. Because of the large number of people seeking initiation into the church at this parish (over 70 people are in their initiation process at any one time), they have had to look for ways to make their group smaller, particularly at ritual celebrations.

One way they have approached this issue is by allowing natural distinctions to define the groups (time of year when they enter the process, baptismal status, whether they are entering individually or as a family). From the very start, team members are clear about the potential settings for the celebration of full initiation. Catechumens celebrate the initiation sacraments at the Easter Vigil; candidates do so at some other time during the year (such as on the Feast of Christ the King or some other appropriate Sunday). It is only by exception that a candidate will be received into full communion during the Easter Vigil. Thus right from the start, the baptized person is awakened to a difference in his or her life. Although at first some candidates for reception feel that it diminishes the importance of the process they are undergoing, in the course of the initiation process and their eventual celebration of reception they realize the grace of their baptism and are thankful for the parish's approach.

During the precatechumenate period, the inquiry team at St. Philip draws on the baptized candidates' experience and knowledge of the Christian story to help evangelize the inquirers who do not have any Christian background. This helps the candidates develop a sense of reverence for what they bring as baptized Christians, and it aids the team in discerning the candidates' level of catechetical formation.

St. Augustine in Washington, D.C., has a special gathering with the baptized inquirers as part of their discernment process in preparation for the rite of welcome. During this session, the catechumenate team and sponsors join the inquirers to help them reflect on what entering into the next period of pastoral formation means for them. As a part of this reflection time, they explore how their baptism will be the foundation of their coming formation.

Two Canadian parishes, St. Vincent de Paul in Weyburn, Saskatchewan, and Holy Cross in Regina, Saskatchewan, shared stories that illustrate ecumenical sensitivity. At St. Vincent during the precatechumenate, the formation team spends time with the baptized inquirers explaining why the Catholic church accepts their baptism and expressing thanks for those who had them baptized. During the celebration of the Rite of Welcoming Candidates, Holy Cross parish makes specific reference to the Christian communities in which the candidates have been baptized. Shortly after this celebration, a letter is sent to each baptized candidate's church of origin thanking them for the initial formation they provided. (Although the formation team wished to do this for each baptized Christian, most often they were only able to do it for those who were at least somewhat catechized and had some sense of prior affiliation with their community of baptism.)

Almost all the parishes I interviewed involve the baptized candidates in the Sunday dismissal. Several respondents indicated, however, that they approach the candidates regarding the question of participation in the Sunday dismissal with sensitivity to their baptismal status. Although the catechumens were expected to participate, the team would offer the candidates an invitation to participate. Some teams did this individually, while others called the candidates together specifically to explore the question. In each approach, an explanation was given of both the purpose of the dismissal and the reason they were being invited rather than expected to participate. In the majority of cases, the candidates accepted the invitation.

Two parishes, St. John Francis Regis in Kansas City, Missouri, and Most Holy Trinity in San Jose, California, indicated that it is their practice not to include the candidates in the Sunday dismissal. They see this as a way of fostering the candidates' respect for their baptism. Because the candidates are baptized, they can participate in the prayers of the faithful and have a place at the table of the Lord as active participants in the eucharistic prayer.

Three geographically different parishes, St. Augustine in Washington, D.C., St. Louise in Bellevue, Washington, and St. Marcelline in Schaumburg, Illinois, each occasionally divide their catechumenate group into smaller groups based on baptismal status (St. Augustine and St. Marcelline usually break them into two groups, unbaptized and baptized; St. Louise creates three groups: the unbaptized; the baptized, uncatechized; and the baptized, somewhat catechized). This breaking down into smaller groups usually occurs when the rhythm of the parish's life offers a "teachable moment" regarding baptism (for example, when infant baptism is celebrated at Mass, on the feast of the Baptism of the Lord or when the readings speak about baptism).

Questions for reflection and discussion are developed to explore baptism from each group's reference point (What does it mean to you as you approach baptism? What difference do you recognize in your life because of your baptism? What does your baptism mean to you? How is your baptism affecting your life?). When the topic permits, St. Louise parish includes questions for the somewhat catechized group that seek to explore how the candidates' communities of origin approach a particular issue, tradition or ritual. Similarities and differences between the Catholic church and the candidates' original communities are reviewed to help clarify and build on the foundation already laid.

After sufficient time in these smaller groups, everyone regathers for some large-group sharing. This method of meeting first in smaller groups and then gathering in the large group is also used at other times in the weekly catechetical sessions. This allows each group to focus on the given topic from the perspective of their approaching or already accomplished baptism.

REFLECTIONS ON THE PASTORAL RESPONSES

In my opinion, people like Mark, who come to the point of wishing they hadn't already been baptized, do so because of two things most initiation teams do: One is an act of commission, the other an act of omission. The first is what the team projects as the pinnacle of initiation, and the second is the failure to dedicate time and energy to discovering the baptisms already celebrated.

What Is the Pinnacle of Initiation?

When working with a combined group of catechumens and candidates, initiation ministers often speak about the culmination of the initiation process in these or similar words: "When you are baptized at the Easter Vigil . . ." Whenever we say something like this, we inadvertently communicate that baptism is the pinnacle of the initiation journey. This reflects the understanding prevalent in the church at the time of the writing of *Christian Initiation: General Introduction,* which is printed in the front of both the *Rite of Baptism for Children* and the *Rite of Christian Initiation of Adults.* In the *General Introduction,* initiation is usually referred to by the singular sacrament of baptism (for example, "Offices and Ministries of Baptism" is one of the subheadings in the document).

The *Rite of Christian Initiation of Adults* indicates a further development in the church's understanding of initiation. The introductory notes for this document usually refer to the whole experience of the catechumenate process (e.g., "the initiation of catechumens" [#4] ; "the rite of initiation" [#5]) or to the three sacraments of baptism, confirmation and eucharist (e.g., "the celebration of the sacraments of Christian initiation" [#23]). When the document addresses the actual celebration of the initiation sacraments, it says:

> The third step in the Christian initiation of adults is the celebration of the sacraments of baptism, confirmation and eucharist. Through this final step the elect, receiving pardon for their sins, are admitted into the people of God. They are graced with adoption as children of God and are led by the Holy Spirit into the promised fullness of time begun in Christ and, as they share in the eucharistic sacrifice and meal, even to a foretaste of the kingdom of God. (#206 U.S., 198 Can.)

Addressing the neophytes' first sharing in the eucharist, the order says:

> Finally in the celebration of the eucharist, as they take part for the first time and with full right, the newly baptized reach the culminating point in their Christian initiation. (#217 U.S., 210 Can.)

Thus we can see that the adult order shifts the focus from the water bath of baptism to the eating and drinking at the Lord's table in eucharist as the pinnacle of the journey. Such a shift is more in keeping with the vision presented in the Second Vatican Council's *Constitution on the Sacred Liturgy (Sacrosanctum Concilium)*:

> The liturgy is the summit toward which the activity of the church is directed; at the same time it is the fount from which all the church's power flows. For the aim and object of apostolic works is that all who are made children of God by faith and baptism should come together to praise God in the midst of his church, to take part in the sacrifice, and to eat the Lord's Supper.

The liturgy in its turn moves the faithful, filled with "the paschal sacraments," to be "one in holiness" (#10).

It is more appropriate, then, for initiation ministers to focus on unity at the table rather than on baptism, to speak of joining us at the eucharistic table rather than of being baptized. In so doing, the emphasis is shifted from a one-time event (baptism), which some have already celebrated, to a repeatable event (eucharist) toward which all are moving. Such a shift in emphasis not only avoids diminishing respect for the candidates' baptism but also helps the entire catechumenal group see their initiation as the first step in a process that does not stop at the font of baptism—it continues on through the period of mystagogy and all of life, nurtured and sustained at the eucharistic table.

Discovering One's Baptism

Although I came across some different ways that parishes help baptized candidates reflect on particular issues in light of their baptism, I did not come across any parish that helps them to discover their actual baptism. It seems reasonable to assume that it would be difficult for an uncatechized person to talk about the effects of baptism in his or her life if that person hasn't spent some time getting in touch with the actual occasion of his or her baptism. Because most candidates' baptisms occurred when they were infants or very young children, most of them will have little or no awareness of the event. As a result, reverence for one's baptism is a concern that can be addressed only after knowledge of it has been attained. A part of our formation task, therefore, is to help the candidate discover his or her baptism and then foster reverence for it.

Since the baptized inquirer needs to show some written testimony of being baptized as part of the precatechumenate work, why not make this an opportunity to do something creative: Instead of just having the inquirer produce proof of baptism, invite the person to do a little discovery about it. Perhaps he or she could collect stories from relatives who remember the event, contact godparents, gather pictures of the celebration, visit the church and locate the font. Sponsors should be prepared to help in the discovery and to listen to the story as it evolves.

Prior to celebrating the rite of welcome, have a gathering just for the baptized inquirers who are ready and their sponsors. Plan the session as a time for reflection and sharing rather than for formal catechesis. Gather at the baptismal font, if possible, or establish a prayerful setting elsewhere using water and a lit candle as a centerpiece. During this session, allow each person to share what he or she has discovered. Include prayers of thanksgiving for those who had the inquirers baptized and for the Christian community within which they entered their relationship with Christ and his people. A blessing with the water as a reminder of their baptism could conclude the session.

One of the parish leaders should make notations of the baptismal information, but the written documents should be kept by the inquirer to be used later in the initiation process (see chapter 7).

When specific attention is not given to developing the uncatechized candidates' respect for their baptism, we should not be surprised when they react negatively to the adapted rites by feeling either left out or like second-class citizens. When we hear such responses we should look less to the flaws in the proposed adapted rites and more to the flaws in our own approach. The rites presume an understanding of and a respect for the baptism already celebrated. The question "How are we as initiation ministers working to foster the candidates' respectful awareness of their baptism?" may be a more appropriate question for catechumenate teams to explore than "How can we reform these adapted rites to be more egalitarian in the way they include the candidates?"

ABOUT THE DISMISSAL

As you have just read, there are different approaches to the question of whether or not to dismiss the candidates from the Sunday eucharistic assembly. The U.S. edition of the ritual text is ambiguous regarding whether or not the candidates are to be dismissed from the Sunday assembly. It says neither that they should be nor that they should not be. The reader can infer, however, that the preference is toward that they should not be. At the end of the adapted rite of welcome (#432–433, U.S. only), it is clear that the rite presumes either that the entire assembly is being dismissed (as at the end of a specially arranged liturgy of the word) or that everyone, including the newly welcomed candidates, is remaining for the liturgy of the eucharist. At the end of the combined rites of acceptance and welcome, two options are presented for when the eucharist is to be celebrated: Either the catechumens are dismissed (#528A and B, U.S. only) or the catechumens remain in the assembly because for "serious reasons they cannot leave" (#538C, U.S. only). What the candidates are to do, however, is not mentioned. Presumably they remain with the assembly, as appears to be the case when the rite of welcome alone is celebrated.

The Canadian text takes an opposite and more definite stance when, as a part of the Rite of Welcoming the Candidates, just *after* the prayers of the faithful and before indicating that "the liturgy of eucharist begins as usual," it states:

> Candidates for reception into the full communion of the Catholic church are invited to leave the assembly together with their catechist, in order to reflect further upon God's word. (#485, Can. only)

Why this discrepancy? Because this is new territory. It is another aspect of our still-developing ecumenical sensitivity (about which both Rita Ferrone and Joseph Favazza have written in previous chapters). This rubric recognizes that by virtue of their baptism, candidates for reception into full communion have a responsibility for intercessory prayer and a place at the eucharistic table. At the same time, however, because of ecclesial separation, they cannot participate in the eucharistic sharing, which for us signifies union. Thus, they do and do not have a place at the eucharistic table, and therein lies the ambiguity within the U.S. text and the discrepancy between the U.S. and Canadian editions.

So should the candidates be dismissed? I favor offering them the invitation and exploring the issue with them so that they can make an informed decision. One of the goals of the renewal of the liturgy is to see proclaiming the prayer of thanksgiving and sharing in the meal as two parts of one eucharistic action. The preferred demeanor for those who are present at the eucharist is full, conscious and active participation. Thus if one is not able to participate in the action, it is inappropriate to be a passive bystander. (Isn't that why we dismiss the catechumens—because they cannot participate?) The candidates, by virtue of their baptism, are able to participate in the eucharistic prayer, but by virtue of the discipline of the Catholic church, not in the eucharistic sharing. Should they be dismissed after the eucharistic prayer and prior to the communion rites (which begin with the Lord's Prayer)? To what avail? Should they be left to stand by and watch others eat, thus being formed in a passive spirituality about the eucharist? I opt for providing them with an opportunity for formation in which they can participate fully and actively by continuing with the liturgy of the word in the dismissal session.

QUESTION: PASTORAL FORMATION

As one begins to take seriously the order's mandate for developing a catechesis that is suitable to the individuals entering into the initiation process, two questions are bound to arise. First, should the formation of baptized candidates (whether uncatechized or catechized) be done separately from or together with the catechumens, and second, what should guide the formation offered?

PASTORAL RESPONSES

Almost all the parishes interviewed include the baptized, uncatechized candidates in the parish's catechumenate rather than offering a separate initiation process for them. In these cases, the catechesis provided is usually based on one of three sources: the questions about Catholic teachings and practice that the catechumenate team draws out of the Sunday readings (mindful of the catechumens and candidates), the questions the catechumens and candidates raise after reflecting on the Sunday readings, or the syllabus designed either by a parish leader or by the author of some book. In most cases, the emphasis tended to be on formation through information rather than transformation. As parishes began to focus more on the Sunday word than on a chapter of a selected book, however, the transformation could not be contained. Many of the leaders interviewed expressed a shift in their own understanding of and approach to initiation and so were beginning to focus more on fostering the conversion God was prompting in the lives of the catechumens and candidates.

Only one parish provides a separate formation experience. At Most Holy Trinity in San Jose, California, two team members journey along with any baptized candidates and their sponsors. In this situation, catechesis is designed in response to the needs discerned during the precatechumenate period.

REFLECTIONS ON THE PASTORAL RESPONSES

Separate or Together?

The ritual text is ambiguous regarding the issue of whether candidates should be formed with the catechumens or in a separate group.

Although the text makes a number of statements in which it likens the formation of baptized, uncatechized persons to that of catechumens (see #401, 402, 406, 407, 408 U.S.; 377, 378, 382, 383, 384 Can.), it does not state that their formation should be done either separately or together. Only in the U.S. edition do we find any statement directly supporting a combined formation:

> Those who have been baptized but have received relatively
> little Christian upbringing may participate in the elements
> of catechumenal formation so far as necessary and appro-
> priate. (National Statutes, #31 U.S. only)

The inclusion of "Appendix I: Additional (Combined) Rites" (U.S. only), however, appears to presume that the formation is done together and leads to ritual steps celebrated together. But the case can be made that although the formation sessions during a given period are to be done separately, the liturgical rites are to be celebrated in combined form.

The question, then, is an open issue. In almost all parishes, the available personnel resources and the time available lead the catechumenate teams to decide that formation together is the better plan. When such is the choice, I believe it is important for the catechumenate team to remember that the catechesis for baptized candidates is mystagogical, i.e., postbaptismal. As the rite says:

> In the process of catechesis the priest, deacon, or catechist
> should take into account that these adults have a special sta-
> tus because they are already baptized. (#402 U.S., 378 Can.)

Thus, this is a time "during which the faith infused in baptism must grow in them and take deep root through the pastoral formation they receive" (#401 U.S., 377 Can.).

If the normal approach is to have combined gatherings, one way to address this is to augment the entire process at various times. Dividing the group for reflection and discussion according to baptismal status (as St. Augustine, St. Marcelline and St. Louise parishes do) is one practice that I would recommend. In addition, having whole sessions from time to time just for the baptized candidates allows the team to address specific issues, concerns and questions focusing on the effects of baptism within their lives. Periodically including such separate discussions and sessions can help the candidates recognize the benefits of their baptism and allow its importance to take root within them.

Guide for Catechesis

When considering the appropriate catechesis for candidates, we must reckon first and foremost with the fact that the catechesis we provide the candidates is postbaptismal, that is, mystagogical. Our starting point is their baptism. A major thrust of the catechesis needs to be unfolding this mystery—this sacrament—in their lives, helping them become aware of its effects. Mark Searle sets me thinking when at the end of chapter 4 he writes:

> If it were only one's inner life with God that counted, sacraments would be nothing more than private "means of grace," supports for an ongoing interior life. But just as character implies grace, so grace implies character. In other words, a [baptized] person's relationship to God is always in Christ and in the church, and it seeks expression in the social role identified with *character:* an ecclesial vocation to participate in Christ's work of mediating between God and humanity, in publicly acknowledging the name of God in worship and in bringing the gifts of God to the world for which they are destined.

My experience with baptized, uncatechized adults is often that although their inner life has lacked any formal spirituality, they have had some sense of the transcendent, the divine, the sacred. Often their outward life is very christianized. Could it be that although they have been, for all practical purposes, unaware of their baptism, it has been having an effect on their way of life? Is their sense of charity, for example, merely humanistic, or does it emanate from a deeper Christian reality within them that seeks expression in the social realm?

If what Searle says is true, it provides us with a guide to their catechesis. Unlike the mystagogical reflections that take place after ritual celebrations during the catechumenate process, in these cases it is not a matter of unfolding the meaning of baptism from the vantage point of the sacramental action (which they do not remember); rather, it is an unfolding of the meaning of baptism from the lived experiences of the candidates. Where in the various significant and not so significant events of their lives do they see the effects of their baptism being made manifest? Where have they been participating "in Christ's work of mediating between God and humanity, in publicly acknowledging the name of God in worship and in bringing the gifts of God to the world for which they are destined"? How has this wellspring within them been a source of nourishment in their lives? This is a part of what those parishes are doing when they periodically gather the candidates by themselves or have the candidates gather together in a smaller group during a combined session to discuss a question developed specifically to help them address the issue or topic at hand from the vantage point of their baptism.

But only looking back is not sufficient. We are not seeking to create spiritual nostalgia. We look back to draw inspiration, understanding and conviction—all of this reflection on what has preceded is the foundation for what is to follow. Thus, as a part of this mystagogical catechesis, we must follow through and ask what is being prompted within them now as a result of a new-found responsiveness to God. What activity is the grace of baptism moving them toward? In light of the responses to these questions, the task is to draw from the church's treasury of teachings and practices to support and nurture as full a response as possible.

Providing rites during this formation period also is important. Because the U.S. edition doesn't provide any models for this, catechumenate teams in the U.S. usually rely on some or all of the rites belonging to the period of the catechumenate (#81–105 U.S.). Great caution needs to be taken with this—some, though not all, of the prayers and rites are pointedly prebaptismal. In contrast, the Canadian text includes a well-crafted and important section in appendix III, "Other Rites for Use in Canada." The section titled "Rites During the Period of Christian Formation" (#488–493, Can. only) includes "Prayers for Strength" (in place of the minor exorcisms) and "Prayers of Blessing" (developed specifically for baptized candidates). In the *praenotanda* for each of these sections, the *Book of Blessings*, an official ritual book for the Catholic Church (published in Canada by the Canadian Conference of Catholic Bishops and in the United States by Catholic Book Publishing Company and The Liturgical Press), is recommended as a source for other appropriate rites.

CONCLUSION

Although it is true in most cases that the uncatechized Christian is much like the unbaptized person where catechetical formation is concerned, we must remember two things: First, by virtue of the baptism already celebrated, their status is different; and second, any catechetical formation we will provide is postbaptismal. Therefore, when considering the formation of the uncatechized Christian, we will always do well to think mystagogically!

CHAPTER SEVEN

Final Preparation of Uncatechized Christians

RONALD A. OAKHAM

This penitential rite can serve to mark the Lenten purification of baptized but previously uncatechized adults who are preparing to receive the sacraments of confirmation and eucharist or to be received into the full communion of the Catholic church. (#459, U.S.)

This penitential rite may also help to prepare the candidates to celebrate the sacrament of penance. (#461, U.S.)

During the season of Lent, penance services may be celebrated on one or more occasions with baptized Catholics who are completing their initiation, and with baptized Christians coming into the full communion of the church. (#522, Can.)

Penitential services will foster a spirit of penance in the candidates and help them prepare to celebrate the sacrament of reconciliation before the completion of their initiation. (#523, Can.)

For the most part, having catechumens and uncatechized candidates for full communion participate in the same process and the same ritual celebrations during the pre-catechumenate and catechumenate does not pose many problems or conflicts. This is especially true in the United States, where the ritual text provides a combined form of the rites of acceptance and welcome (#505–529, U.S. only). Problems begin to arise, however, during the shift from the catechumenate period into the time of purification and enlightenment.

With the parish rites of sending (#536–546, U.S. only) and the diocesan rites of election and call to continuing conversion (#547–561, U.S. only), the ritual distinctions carry considerable weight. In these rites the distinction is borne out not only with changes in language but also with directives about who can partake in various aspects of the rites (for example, who signs the Book of the Elect). In Canada, where the ritual text does not include combined rites, the distinctions are drawn even more clearly. The introductory notes regarding the adapted rite of calling candidates to Lenten renewal (#494–509, Can. only) indicate very clearly that it is not to be celebrated with the rite of election (#497, Can. only).

In both the U.S. and Canadian texts, there is no combined rite for the scrutinies. The texts are consistent in their view that these rites, which culminate in the prayers of exorcism, are pre-baptismal and thus for the unbaptized only; penitential rites and the sacrament of penance are the appropriate rituals for the baptized.

During Lent, catechumenate teams may come to know whether they have built up or diminished baptized candidates' respect for their baptism (see the opening story of chapter 6). In addition, it is in regard to the rites of this period that the most controversy exists among catechumenate ministers, both in parishes and in the national leadership. It is a good tension, though, spurring critical study and thought regarding new questions within our church. As Rita Ferrone indicated in chapter 2, we are dealing with initiation issues within a milieu that is unique in our church's history. Our post–Vatican II thoughts about, awareness of and sensitivity toward ecumenical issues have brought us to a new understanding of ourselves and our relationship with our Christian sisters and brothers in other communities. As a result, we have adapted some of our initiation rites and have created others to accommodate these new understandings. But are the given rites adequate?

Many feel, as I do, that what is provided is not sufficient. But what more is needed? Some propose adapting the Lenten scrutinies to include the baptized candidates.[1] Others, however, suggest that there are various rites within our liturgical treasury that are more appropriate. Thus, rather than adapting the scrutinies, we should look to these other rites, dust them off and give them renewed life. It is from this position that I will consider the question in this chapter.

PASTORAL RESPONSES

QUESTION: CALLING CANDIDATES
TO CONTINUING CONVERSION

Most parishes interviewed indicated that they celebrate the call to continuing conversion as presented in the liturgical text. St. Philip in Bakersfield, California, however, has made an interesting adaptation. As noted in the previous chapter, this parish celebrates the reception of baptized Christians at times other than the Easter Vigil. Thus, they do not celebrate the call to continuing conversion in combination with the rite of election, nor is it a diocesan celebration — which is not required for baptized candidates — but a parish celebration.

The initiation team at St. Philip sought to build on the ritual gesture of signing the Book of the Elect in the adapted rite, but they did not want to imitate this gesture. Instead, they have incorporated the baptismal certificates or other documentation that the candidates acquired during the precatechumenate period.

The rite is celebrated at a Sunday Mass with the entire catechumenal community present. The Sunday selected is the one with the most appropriate readings around six weeks prior to the Sunday on which reception will be celebrated. The rite occurs after the readings and homily, and it follows the ritual text for the affirmation by the sponsors (#452B U.S., 502B Can.) and assembly (#453 U.S., 502 Can.). After exhorting the sponsors to continue their support of the candidates, the presider invites the candidates to present their baptismal certificates: "As evidence of your baptism within another Christian community, and as a sign of your intention to enter into the full communion of the Catholic church, please present your baptismal certificate to us." The catechumenate director calls the names of the candidates, and they are led forward by their sponsors.

The assembly sings a setting of "There is one Lord, one faith, one baptism" during the procession and presentation. A member of the initiation team receives the certificates, placing them in a prepared book, and the candidates gather together in the altar area, facing the assembly. The book is then placed on a stand near the baptismal font, and the paschal candle is lighted. (This display will remain in place throughout this final preparation period.) The presider then proclaims the act of recognition (#454 U.S., 503 Can.), which is followed by the intercessions and prayer over the candidates.

In concluding the rite, the other members of the catechumenal community are called forward, and all are blessed and dismissed. The newly "recognized" candidates gather as a separate group from now on, since the focus of their sessions will be to help them spiritually prepare for their reception into the church.

QUESTION: PURIFICATION AND ENLIGHTENMENT

When the final period of preparation for sacramental initiation occurs during Lent, very little is done to address the unique situation of baptized candidates. Because the parish's leadership is concerned with Lenten programs, the scrutinies and presentations, and preparations for the Triduum, the baptized candidates are often just swept up into these dynamics. From the responses of the various parishes, two patterns emerged: Either the Lenten rites were adapted to include the baptized, or the baptized celebrated the adapted penitential rite (#464–472, U.S. only) or penitential services (#522–527, Can. only) separate from the scrutiny celebrations. These penitential rituals may or may not have been presented as an integral step leading to a celebration of the sacrament of penance (more on this celebration later).

Only one parish reported that it was doing something that addressed the issue of baptized candidates at the scrutinies. St. Louise parish in Bellevue, Washington, did not celebrate the penitential rite given in the ritual text, nor did they adapt the language of the scrutinies to include the baptized. Instead, the baptized candidates joined with the rest of the baptized assembly during the celebration of the scrutiny rites and prayed over the unbaptized. One adaptation of the rite was made to recognize the unique relationship that the baptized candidates had developed with the elect during their catechumenal formation: After the elect were called forward with their godparents, the candidates were invited forward. They each stood near one of the elect so that each of the elect had one or more candidates nearby. During the part of the exorcism prayer that calls for a laying on of hands, the candidates, in addition to the presider and godparents, laid hands on the elect by whom they were standing. As a part of the reflection on the rites, the group explored the experience and its meaning for both the elect and the candidates.

Several parishes celebrated this "period of more intense spiritual preparation" outside the context of Lent. In these cases, special attention and care had to be given to developing something specifically for the baptized candidates.

Mary, Mother of the Church parish in St. Louis, Missouri, had one candidate ready for reception in the fall. After celebrating the call to continuing conversion within the parish, the candidate spent a retreat-like period of several weeks, with a catechist and her sponsor, preparing for reception into full communion. The Sunday readings were used for the reflection sessions on Sundays; at a separate gathering during the week, the Creed was used to guide the prayer and reflection.

At St. Marcelline in Schaumburg, Illinois, a six-week retreat-like period is developed using the regular Sunday readings for that time. The weekly sessions consist of guided meditations and reflections along with a prayer experience which uses one of the symbols of initiation. Each aspect of this period is developed to complement each other one, so that together they form a single path leading to the celebration of reception. Only one penitential rite, modeled on the Lenten scrutiny (as was the penitential rite in the U.S. edition), is celebrated.

The prayer over the candidates was written by the parish liturgist following the structure of the exorcism prayers but drawing on the imagery of the readings for that Sunday.

St. Philip parish focuses its period of preparation on a renewal of baptismal promises in preparation for reception into the church. In addition to the separate gathering at the Sunday dismissal sessions, the candidates preparing for reception and their sponsors gather for weekly evening sessions. The first session explores the church's understanding of baptism and mission, and builds on the candidates' current understanding of these two topics.

The next three sessions were developed using William Reiser's *Renewing the Baptismal Promises* (see the bibliography for a full reference). Each session focuses on one of the baptismal renunciations of sin paired with one of the questions that form the profession of faith: First, Do you reject Satan, father of sin and prince of darkness, and, Do you believe in God, the Father almighty, creator of heaven and earth? Second, Do you reject Satan and all his works, and, Do you believe in Jesus Christ? Third, Do you reject Satan's empty promises, and, Do you believe in the Holy Spirit? Rather than offering lectures on the theological underpinnings of each statement, the evenings' presenters offer images that portray each question and help the candidates relate the questions to their own lives.

The fifth week's gathering begins with an open discussion about the images, ideas and notions the candidates have about the church's penance practices. This is followed by some dispelling of any erroneous understandings as well as by sharing from some sponsors and team members about their experience of reconciliation in the church. In these sessions, the sponsors and team focus more on the church's mission as reconciler than on the sacrament of penance. The evening concludes with a penitential service (not the sacrament of penance) that includes an examen developed from the previous reflections on the baptismal promises.

A prayer service that includes a celebration of the ephphetha rite completes the last evening's reflection on what the candidates have been hearing in the proclaimed word, how it has taken flesh in their lives and how they can be better proclaimers of this word. On the Saturday morning preceding the Sunday celebration of reception, the sponsors gather for a rehearsal; after the rehearsal, they gather with the candidates and their families for a time of prayer that is a celebration of their renewal of baptismal promises.

QUESTION: SACRAMENT OF PENANCE

St. Louise parish (where the candidates join the rest of the baptized in praying for the elect at the scrutinies) culminates their Lenten time with the candidates with a session just for the baptized candidates. This session was designed as an evening retreat focused on an examination of conscience as a way of preparing for celebrating penance. During this session, some of the candidates celebrate the sacrament individually with one of the parish priests. Others celebrate the sacrament at the parish's Lenten celebration, during which several priests are available for individual confession and absolution. During this parish celebration, some of the reflections offered by the candidates as a part of the examination of conscience are woven into the examination presented to the parish assembly.

As part of its usual schedule of prayer, St. Marcelline offers the individual celebration of the sacrament of penance weekly and a communal celebration with individual confession and absolution monthly. When candidates are in the final preparation period for reception into the church, they are prepared for and celebrate the sacrament at the monthly communal celebration.

St. Philip parish has altered the way they celebrate penance with their candidates. Formerly, they celebrated the sacrament at a communal celebration with individual confession and absolution as a ritual conclusion to the weekly gathering at which they explored the church's mission of reconciliation. They discontinued this practice for two reasons: First, they felt that by doing it in this setting they were creating a situation that forced the candidates into celebrating the sacrament;

second, the celebration ended in a frayed and individual manner. Currently, they conclude that evening with a penitential prayer service. After the prayer time, a brief instruction about the sacrament is given along with a presentation on the options available to them for its celebration (during the regularly scheduled time each week, by appointment or after the prayer service on the Saturday prior to the Sunday celebration).

St. Augustine parish in Washington, D.C., includes a reconciliation celebration in their three-day Lenten retreat for the elect and candidates. All are invited to be present for the celebration using the communal form with individual confession and absolution. Prior to the rite, an instruction is given that emphasizes that the elect will be reconciled in the waters of baptism, and an invitation is extended to the candidates to participate fully in the sacrament, emphasizing that doing so is their free choice. The elect and candidates also are invited to participate in the parish's communal penance celebration during Holy Week. Some of the candidates who don't celebrate the sacrament during the retreat take this opportunity to do so.

St. John Francis Regis previously included the opportunity to celebrate the sacrament individually as a part of a retreat day during Lent, but they have discontinued this practice. Now, at the end of an evening focused on reconciliation, they encourage the candidates to participate in the parish's communal penance celebration (with individual penance and absolution) during Holy Week.

During the fifth week of Lent, St. Mary parish in Buffalo Grove, Illinois, has a communal penance celebration (with individual penance and absolution) specifically prepared for adults and children who are candidates for reception into the church, older children who haven't celebrated first penance and Catholics who are reuniting with the church through the parish's ministry of reconciliation with alienated Catholics. Family members, sponsors, team members and catechists from the various groups also are invited to participate. At the time for individual confession and absolution, various confessors take their places around the church, where they then hear the confessions of the participants (instrumental music is played during this time so that the penitents' voices cannot be heard by the rest of the assembly). After confessing and being absolved, participants wait in silent prayer until all who have desired to celebrate the sacrament fully have completed their turn. The ritual concludes with a prayer of praise and thanksgiving, a blessing, a dismissal and a closing hymn.

REFLECTION ON THE PASTORAL RESPONSES

In describing the season of Lent, the *General Norms for the Liturgical Year and Calendar* says:

> Lent is a preparation for the celebration of Easter. For the Lenten liturgy disposes both catechumens and the faithful to celebrate the paschal mystery: catechumens, through the several stages of Christian initiation; the faithful, through reminders of their own baptism and through penitential practices.[2]

The *Rite of Christian Initiation of Adults* builds on this statement when in an introductory paragraph and in the presider's words to the candidates it states:

> In the liturgy and liturgical catechesis of Lent the reminder of baptism already received or the preparation for its reception, as well as the theme of repentance, renew the entire community along with those being prepared to celebrate the paschal mystery. (#138 U.S., 125 Can.)

> Join with us this Lent in a spirit of repentance. Hear the Lord's call to conversion and be faithful to your baptismal covenant. (#454, U.S. only)

> We invite you to be one with us during this Lenten season. By prayer, fasting, and works of charity, we will unite ourselves more closely to Christ. (#503, Can. only)

The penitential character of Lent, then, becomes the character of this final period of preparation. The remainder of this chapter will explore two points regarding this final period: the place of the baptized candidate in the Lenten rites and the final preparation that occurs outside Lent.

PLACE OF THE BAPTIZED CANDIDATE

It seems, at first, that the baptized referred to in paragraphs #138 (U.S. edition) and #125 (Canadian edition) are primarily the parish members (i.e., the faithful). But with our post – Vatican II ecumenical awareness, we recognize that this statement includes anyone who is one with us in baptism and is participating in our community life to some degree, especially, in this context, baptized candidates who are preparing to enter into the full communion of the Catholic church.

Thus a number of initiation ministers believe that the baptized candidates' path to the Triduum celebration of the paschal mystery should follow and be modeled on the penitential journey prescribed for the fully initiated, baptized Catholic;[3] others propose extending the inclusivity of the existing initiatory rites of Lent prescribed for catechumens. I agree with Jim Dunning's position that what is needed is more, not less, ritual for the uncatechized, baptized candidates.[4] But I disagree with his recommendation that we include them in the prebaptismal rituals. I believe, rather, that we should implement other rites that lay fallow or develop additional, appropriate rituals when they do not exist within our treasury of rites. From this point of view, let us look at the transitional rites of election and call to continuing conversion, and at the scrutiny and penitential rites.

Rites of Election and Call to Continuing Conversion

The final period of preparation for baptism usually coincides with the season of Lent and begins with a transitional rite, the rite of election (#129–137 U.S., 116–124 Can.), which celebrates God's action of choosing the candidate for baptism as God's own. To mark this transition for the baptized candidate, an adapted rite was developed — the rite of calling the candidates to continuing conversion, (#446–458, U.S. only) or, in the Canadian text, the rite of calling the candidates to Lenten renewal (#498–509 Can. only). The commissions that adapted the rite of election for use with baptized candidates were mindful of the character and dynamics of Lent and sensitive to the effects of baptism already celebrated. Throughout the ritual, references are made to the candidates' deepening appreciation for and increasing fidelity to their baptism as the foundation for their entering into conversion. This conversion is a turning to God again, a conforming of their lives more and more to the pattern of Christ. It is paschal in nature: dying to that which is not Christlike and rising anew. Only by entering into such a passover can any baptized person truly renew their baptism.

Although intended to be used at the beginning of Lent, this adapted rite is appropriate for beginning the final period of preparation even if it occurs outside of Lent. Whenever it is celebrated, this rite suffers from the same problem as the Rite of Election itself: It is exceptionally verbal. The framers of the Rite of Election tried to compensate for this problem by including the signing of the Book of the Elect, but there is no suggested action in the adapted rite. To remedy this, many parishes invite the candidates to sign the Book of the Elect. The decision for this inclusion is most often based on the idea that election merely signifies preparation for Catholic church membership and simply marks another stage in this journey. Because we often "sign on the dotted line" to indicate our entry into an agreement or relationship, the signing of the Book of the Elect is often seen as a gesture of intent on the part of the one who signs.

But what does signing the book symbolize? This is not an easy question to answer because, like all symbols, it has many levels of meaning. Some initiation ministers favor the understanding that the ancient practice of presenting the names of catechumens ready for full initiation symbolized a willingness of the catechumens to surrender themselves to Christ within the faith community and its covenant relationship. In using the gesture of signing a book as a symbol of giving over one's name, they see the ancient practice given a contemporary twist. When applied to the baptized candidate, it is nuanced to mean surrendering one's self to the Catholic community.

Other initiation ministers favor regarding the Book of the Elect as symbolic of the Book of Life spoken of in the scriptures (Philippians 4:3; Revelations 3:5; 13:8; 17:8; 20:12; 21:27). St. John Chrysostom referred to the book in which the catechumens' names were written as "this heavenly book."[5] Often during reflections on the ritual after its celebration, the catechumens themselves recall these scriptures to name the meaning they see in the gesture. The whole context of the rite's celebration of being chosen by God, becoming one of God's elect, leads to this understanding.

Paul Turner, in a response to Jim Dunning's writings about including the baptized in the prebaptismal rites, proposes another understanding of the signing gesture:

> The rite of election suggests that the unbaptized elect sign the book, but candidates for full communion do not. The liturgy seeks a link between book and water, or more accurately, between name and water. Our names are sacraments of ourselves. They stand for what we stand for. We sign on to ratify, to speak out, to pay our bills, to make the typed words our own. People call us by our name. Election and baptism christianize our names. To call us by name is to call us Christian. Catechumens also have the option of choosing a baptismal name (#200–205 U.S., 187–189 Can.), a ritual which makes sense only if they're changing the name by which they wish to be called for the rest of their lives.
>
> Candidates, however, are in another league altogether. Having been baptized by name, their names already symbolize that they are Christian. At best, the signing of the book is redundant. At worst, it ritually scorns their baptism.[6]

Personally, I find both the idea of the signing as symbolizing one's name being entered into the Book of Life and the idea Paul Turner presents to be the more authentic symbols, rather than the idea of surrendering one's self to the Catholic community. Consequently, I prefer the ritual text's direction that candidates do not sign the book. But, that should not relegate them to being either passive bystanders during election or second-class citizens in the way they are treated within the rite adapted for them.

As baptized persons, candidates for reception already have an active role in the rite of election (and the rite of sending in the U.S. edition). Although focused through the ministry of the godparent, the role of the baptized assembly is to give witness to the action of God within the catechumens' lives, which gives evidence that they are God's chosen ones. If we seek to be more inclusive of the candidates in this ritual, the giving of testimony is what needs to be enhanced in the rite. As baptized members, their proper role is to affirm the testimony given by the godparents and, possibly, to give testimony on behalf of the catechumens.[7]

St. Philip parish's adaptation of the rite of calling the candidates to continuing conversion (described earlier in this chapter) is a commendable example of how this can be done. In a very tangible way, it gives recognition to the baptism already celebrated while at the same time inserting ritual gesture into a very wordy ceremony. What may be needed is an enhancement of the way in which the names are approached within the rite so as to deepen the awareness, both of the candidates and the assembly, of the sacredness of our names as signifying a Christian.

Scrutinies and Penitential Rites

The second concern is (to paraphrase Shakespeare a little): To scrutinize or not to scrutinize? Exorcism is the question! Those who favor including baptized candidates in the prebaptismal rituals maintain that all of us need to scrutinize our lives during Lent as we seek to become better Christians, adding that the prayers need some adapting since they are currently written in prebaptismal imagery. Many who favor this position offer examples of how meaningful their candidates found the rites when the rites were adapted to include them. But is adapting these rites the best approach? To do so assumes that the issue at hand (confronting the evil within our lives) is the same for both unbaptized and baptized. In addressing this question, Paul Turner writes:

> Guideposts for Lent, the scrutinies purify those chosen for baptism. Through exorcisms, they ask God to expel the spirit of evil and fill the elect with the spirit of goodness. Exorcisms presume not demonic possession but that the prebaptismal state more readily concedes to forces of evil. If the initiation rites incorporate new members into the body of Christ, if they fill newcomers with the Holy Spirit, people must pass from some nasty former state to enjoy the fullness of life in Christ.
>
> The ritual still presumes that the unbaptized need big exorcisms — and some little ones along the way (#94) — and that the baptized candidates need prayer for the coming of the Spirit, but not exorcisms for the expulsion of spirits (compare #154 and #470 [U.S.]).[8]

Although difficult to identify exactly (Turner uses the phrase "some nasty former state"), the status of the unbaptized versus that of the baptized is not the same when it comes to the question of the potential influence of evil. Baptism, as the church has taught for centuries and as Mark Searle points out in chapter 4, has an effect. Although it does not eradicate the influence of evil in our lives, it does provide a sacred shelter from within which we can fend off evil's attacks. Additionally, the culminating point of exorcisms is reconciliation through the baptismal bath, which incorporates the catechumen into Christ, our sacred shelter. Exorcisms lead one into the font! Because we are not leading the baptized Christian into the font, to include them in the exorcisms is to set them up for disappointment (see the story at the beginning of chapter 6). If adaptation is a plausible idea concerning the scrutinies, it is not when it comes to baptism. If we adapted baptism to include the candidates, it no doubt would provide a wonderful and meaningful experience for them; however, sacramental integrity, not ritual wonder, is our guide for undertaking adaptation.

Those who adapt the scrutinies to include the baptized candidates do so, it seems, primarily as a result of a combination of two concerns. First, they do not want to deprive the candidates of the richness of these rites. I believe, however, that they have not discovered that the church has other rites with which to lead the candidates on an enriching penitential journey that rightfully culminates not in the waters of baptism but in the laying on of hands in the "second baptism," penance. What is needed is not the adaptation of scrutiny rites but the implementation of penitential rites.

Second, the rationale for adaptation betrays, in my estimation, a lack of understanding of the renewed liturgy. If the rites are not adapted, some contend, the candidates feel left out. But this ignores the fact that the baptized assembly has an active role in the ritual. What, then, is the role of the baptized candidates in these Lenten rites—recipients of the assembly's prayer or doers of that prayer? If they are baptized, their rightful place is to be with those who are praying over the unbaptized. This is why I find the adaptation that St. Louise parish has made to be a better approach than the adaptation of the prayers that includes the candidates as recipients of the assembly's prayer.[9]

This final period of preparation is a time for the candidates to enter into a penitential process. Consequently, even though the ritual text does not envision including candidates in the scrutinies, it does envision providing them with a penitential experience. There is a difference, however, between what the U.S. edition proposes and what the Canadian edition proposes. The U.S. edition suggests celebrating one penitential rite (#459–472, U.S. only), which has been developed using the structure of the scrutinies. Although the text recommends celebrating it on the Second Sunday of Lent or on a Lenten weekday, only form A of the exorcism prayer includes images from that Sunday's gospel reading. Those who have used this rite have found the experience unsatisfactory. The Canadian edition approaches the issue with what has the potential to be a more satisfactory experience (#522–527, Can. only): Instead of offering one adapted rite, it recommends celebrating several penitential rites and provides an outline based on the structure of the penitential services found in appendix II of the *Rite of Penance;* to this it adds a laying on of hands. The Canadian text does not include a fully developed ritual but relies on the creative work of the parish's leadership.

These penitential services of the *Rite of Penance,* which often are overlooked, are intended to help the baptized prepare for the celebration of the sacrament of penance. One of the services included is even designed as a Lenten celebration in preparation for the renewal of baptismal promises. Much can be made of these services, as I suggested in a previous article:

> Lenten "retreat" gatherings could be arranged at different times during the weeks of Lent. The baptized — both the candidates for full communion and those already in full communion — can be led (as are the elect, in their own sessions) through prayerful reflections based on the Sunday readings to a scriptural sense of sin and a desire for reconciliation. These sessions may conclude with a penitential rite. . . .
>
> Those who participate in these Lenten exercises should be encouraged to be present at the scrutinies. During these rites we, the baptized who are experiencing God's reconciling power, will pray for the unbaptized that they may experience this same forgiving, healing and liberating power. As "wounded healers" we stand to witness to this power.[10]

It was disheartening to find that nothing much is being done to provide candidates for reception with a penitential process that truly recognizes their baptism. This is especially true when the final period of preparation coincides with Lent. Either the scrutinies are being adapted to include the candidates as recipients of the community's prayer, or the candidates remain with the baptized members of the assembly (whose own sense of inclusion is minimal). Only St. Louise offered something creative and appropriate. They acknowledged both the baptismal status of the candidates and the relationship between the candidates and the catechumens that develops during their time of mutual formation.

Just as exorcisms culminate in the reconciliation of baptism, penitential services culminate in the reconciliation of penance. Yet case after case demonstrated Joseph Favazza's contention that we suffer from pastoral amnesia when it comes to penance (see chapter 3). I found that even in parishes where a communal form of celebrating the sacrament was offered, most initiation teams presented with reserve rather than excitement the suggestion that candidates participate in the sacrament.

I find it interesting that ministers are enthusiastic about weaving baptized candidates into what are primarily prebaptismal rites, while at the same time they hedge when it comes to involving them in the postbaptismal sacrament of penance. I believe that catechumenate leaders' own lack of renewal regarding this sacrament is the culprit. Far too many of us still see it as an encounter with an almighty judge rather than as a celebration of God's gracious mercy already made manifest in the life of the community and within our own lives. Yet penance is the very sacrament that can ritually touch the reality of the candidates' lives as they move toward reception into the church.

> Historically, penance as a separate sacrament has done two things: First, it has reconciled those who have seriously damaged the communion of the church and who have repented of their sin; and second, it has encouraged the ongoing conversion of believers who are forever stumbling over their weaknesses and failings in Christian commitment. Theologically, penance extends to the sinner in both cases the reconciliation of baptism and moves reconciliation toward completion in the eucharist.[11]

As we noted earlier in this chapter, St. Philip parish used to celebrate a communal penance service with the candidates, sponsors and initiation team but no longer does so primarily because of the frayed ending. I suggest that working with the specific problem—the frayed ending—would have been the better decision. A couple of things could have been done. For example, after a candidate has gone to the confessor and received absolution and has spent some time in reflective prayer, he or she could spend time with his or her sponsor reflecting on the experience of the sacramental celebration as experienced thus far. Then when this section of the celebration is completed, all could regather as an assembly and complete the liturgy. Or, if the group is large, after several have completed the confession and absolution portion, they could gather around the altar with their sponsors and an initiation team member, pray the Lord's Prayer together, receive a blessing and be dismissed.

St. Mary and St. Augustine were the two parishes with the strongest approach to celebrating penance. In these two parishes, sacramental celebrations were arranged specifically for the candidates.

I was one of the confessors at the celebration at St. Mary's. At first I was disturbed that it was being held separate from the parish's penance celebration, which was scheduled one week later. But I found that it was a good decision. The initiation team brought together a number of groups for whom the sacrament of penance was a special part of their spiritual preparation for the Triduum, so there was a real sense of a community gathered in prayer. With the various sponsors, catechists and team members present, the parish community was sufficiently represented and actively participating in the rite. Because there was a good ratio of individual penitents to confessors, the individual confessions and absolutions didn't require an inordinate amount of time, which allowed both for an appropriate amount of interaction between confessor and penitent and for a communal ending to the celebration.

On St. Augustine's retreat, some awkwardness arose for the catechumens because, although they were a part of the liturgy of the word, they were not part of the penance rite. After making clear to them that their reconciliation would take place in the baptismal bath, they were dismissed with a blessing. Given the retreat atmosphere, I could see including something a bit more engaging than the dismissal. For example, while the candidates and their sponsors continued with the sacramental celebration, the catechumens could have been invited to spend some time with their godparents sharing about their old self that has died, what still needs to die and the new life that they have risen to. When the baptized members of the assembly had completed the individual confession and absolution portion of the rite, all could have regathered around the altar (the place to which they are journeying together), prayed the Lord's Prayer, received a blessing and then have been dismissed.

Election and the scrutinies are meaningful rites, but they are not our only rites. I encourage initiation ministers to look deeper into our tradition for treasures that are appropriate for the baptized and to develop those. In this way, they will provide the baptized candidates with rich experiences that honor and build on their baptism.

Outside Lent

Reception into the full communion of the Catholic church is not merely a change in one's ecclesial membership; it is a development or deepening of one's baptismal covenant. When this final period of preparation occurs at a time other than during Lent, we should not forget what has been established for Lent: Penitential practices prepare the baptized for renewing their baptismal commitment. Therefore, this period should always be characterized by a penitential process that aims not just to restore a baptismal commitment (which may be needed in a particular case) but also to enhance or renew it.

Though it is not required, it is good pastoral practice to ritualize the transition from the period of formation into this period of final preparation. The ritual text's rite of calling the candidates to continuing conversion/Lenten renewal provides a starting point for developing an appropriate celebration. The first adaptation that needs to be made is changing the Lenten focus (starting with the ritual's name as given in the Canadian text). Throughout the rite, reference is made to Lent; those who prepare the celebration must look through the entire ritual text and make appropriate changes. For other adaptations to be considered, I refer you to what St. Philip parish has done as described earlier in this chapter.

Both St. Marcelline and St. Philip parishes offer good models, described earlier, for developing the period itself. St. Marcelline draws on the Lenten dynamic (established in the Year A lectionary) of presenting foundational stories for the baptismal symbols (white robe, water, oil, anointing, laying on of hands, new light). Although they use the assigned Sunday readings as the foundation for their time together, the baptismal symbols are used for prayerful reflection with the candidates as a part of their sessions together. This serves a two-fold purpose: first, it opens up the meaning of the candidates' baptism, and second, it prepares them to renew that baptism in the profession of faith at the celebration of their reception. On one of the Sundays during this six-week period, the parish celebrates a penitential rite with the candidates, using the scrutiny structure. The Sunday is usually selected according to the one that has the most appropriate readings for such a celebration.

At St. Philip, the initiation ministers have constructed an experience that focuses on the renewal of baptismal vows. Thus, they have chosen to use the baptismal promises as the primary source for their sessions rather than the symbols. They, too, only celebrate one penitential service, which is based on the model given in appendix II of the *Rite of Penance.*

While the approaches of both St. Marcelline and St. Philip to this period of preparation outside Lent are viable, I prefer the one at St. Philip. I find that using the baptismal promises as the framework for the reflections allows for an experience complementary to Lent, whereas the approach used by St. Marcelline could be experienced as redundant to or as a shadow of Lent.

In addition, focusing on the baptismal promises as St. Philip does offers the possibility of developing several penitential services which would culminate in a sacramental celebration of penance. As a part of the sacramental celebration, after all have received absolution the candidates, along with their sponsors and others participating in the celebration, could gather around or near the baptismal font and renew their baptismal promises. This would provide an experience of what the document *Environment and Art in Catholic Worship* hints at when it suggests the location of the reconciliation chapel: "A room or rooms for the reconciliation of individual penitents may be located near the baptismal area."[12] When the penitent leaves the reconciliation chapel, he or she will immediately encounter the baptismal font and in so doing be reminded of his or her first sacramental reconciliation, which has just been renewed in the sacrament of penance. Such a celebration provides the bridge between this penitential time and the celebration of reception, at which the candidates will profess the Creed with the gathered assembly and make their profession of faith in the church as they become one with us at the table of the Lord.

Approaching this period as a penitential time, and incorporating penitential services as well as sacramental celebrations as integral components, will provide the candidates a good catechetical foundation in the church's understanding and practice of reconciliation and will prepare them for their reception into the full communion of the Catholic church.

CONCLUSION

The appropriateness of a penitential process is rooted in a long-standing tradition of our community. In addition to regarding penance as "second baptism," the church has recognized three forms of reconciliation: The primary form is baptism, the ordinary form is eucharist, and the extraordinary form is penance. Entering into the full communion of the Catholic church is an extraordinary move (it is not something that one does every day). Thus, it is best that the final period of preparation for this move (whether within Lent or at another time) is marked with periodic penitential celebrations which culminate in the extraordinary form of baptismal renewal, penance.

Do not allow yourselves to fall prey to the "pastoral amnesia" that Joseph Favazza wrote about. Penance is not external to the initiation process; it is an intrinsic part of it.

ENDNOTES

1. To explore the thinking behind this position, see James Lopresti, "Scrutinies or Confession?" *Catechumenate: A Journal of Christian Initiation* 9, no. 4 (March 1987): 15–19.

2. *General Norms for the Liturgical Year and Calendar,* #27. This document is one of the introductory documents of the sacramentary.

3. For a more developed presentation on this point, see Ronald Oakham, "Baptized Candidates and the Lenten Rites," *Catechumenate: A Journal of Christian Initiation* 12, no. 6 (November 1990): 18–25.

4. James Dunning, "What Is a Catechized Adult?" *Forum Newsletter* 9, no. 2 (Summer 1992): 1.

5. Rita Ferrone, *On the Rite of Election,* Forum Essays, no. 3 (Chicago: Liturgy Training Publications, 1994), 16.

6. Paul Turner, "Forlorn Yet Privileged: The Case of Candidates," *Forum Newsletter* 11, no. 1 (Winter 1994): 3–4, 10.

7. "When appropriate in the circumstances, the celebrant may also ask the entire assembly to express its approval of the candidates in these or similar words" (#131 U.S., 118 Can.). Although a question seeking a simple response is then given, this could be expanded to allow for particular testimony being given on behalf of the individual catechumens. Given the diocesan setting for election, the circumstances (a large gathering of catechumens) may not be appropriate for this adaptation. When a parish celebrates a rite of sending, however, it could be included.

8. Turner, "Forlorn Yet Privileged: The Case of Candidates," 4. (No reference is given here to the Canadian text; it does not include a penitential prayer for candidates with which to make the suggested comparison.)

9. For another idea for adaptation, see Oakham, "Baptized Candidates and the Lenten Rites," 23–24.

10. Ibid., 22.

11. Robert J. Kennedy, "Baptism, Eucharist, Penance: Theological and Liturgical Connections," in *Reconciliation: The Continuing Agenda* (Collegeville: The Liturgical Press, 1987), 50.

12. Bishops' Committee on the Liturgy, *Environment and Art in Catholic Worship* (Washington, D.C.: National Conference of Catholic Bishops, 1978), #81.

CHAPTER EIGHT

Formation of Catechized Christians

RONALD A. OAKHAM

The baptized Christian is to receive both doctrinal and spiritual preparation, adapted to individual pastoral requirements, for reception into the full communion of the Catholic church. The candidate should learn to deepen an inner adherence to the church, where he or she will find the fullness of his or her baptism.   **(#477 U.S., 391 Can.)**

In the early church, the sacrament of penance was regarded as a "second baptism." St. Ambrose remarked that the church "possesses both water and tears: the water of baptism, the tears of penance." In the case of the baptized who have completed a period of formation and are ready to complete their initiation, the sacrament of penance may occupy a place similar to the sacrament of baptism for the elect.   **(#528 Can.)**

Anyone working with parish initiation ministry has heard objections to the length of the catechumenate process. Some of the complaints are, no doubt, embedded in our society's "immediate gratification" syndrome. We prefer instant responses, fast service, quick resolutions and immediate attention in all facets of life. Thus, when people encounter a process that will take time, frustration ensues (not only among those seeking initiation but also among church ministers, especially the clergy). But to shape an important formation experience such as initiation around these conditioned expectations would be a disservice both to the individuals and to our community.

Many of the objections are rightfully expressed, however. Some of those who come seeking reception into the church may in fact come with a background of catechetical formation that deserves a pastoral response different from the normal parish initiation process (presuming this is the full catechumenate process). The *Rite of Christian Initiation of Adults* never intended, for example, that a Catholic's spouse, who has been participating in the life of the parish for the past 23 years by attending church every Sunday, by being involved in parent preparation sessions for their children's celebration of the sacraments, by contributing to the communal and apostolic dimensions of the parish's life and by generally participating in the church's life, should be required to take part in an extended process of formation. At the same time, however, the revised order of Christian initiation does not anticipate that this person's reception would be celebrated in a way that is individual and quasi-private. In fact, the order expects that attention will be given to the appropriate use of the normative dimensions (written about in chapter 5) that are woven into the initiation process outlined in part I of the ritual text.

The strongest resistance to implementing the order of Christian initiation of adults often is based in an authentic concern for the baptized, *catechized* Christian who comes seeking reception into the church. I see two problems with this resistance. First, catechized Christians are, in my experience, the exception rather than the norm among baptized persons who come to us. More often than not, they are uncatechized. Second, people who have this concern tend to dismiss the entire vision presented in the order rather than striving to implement the vision more completely.

In chapter 1 of this book, Kathy Brown describes what her parish's initiation team has learned, and she offers several cases that illustrate how they learned these things. Her parish, Most Holy Trinity in Phoenix, Arizona, is working toward implementing the vision of Christian initiation more completely, as are several other parishes that have developed ways for journeying with the baptized, catechized Christian.

Before sharing the stories of the other parishes, let's recall the pastoral approaches Kathy Brown wrote about in the stories she shared about several candidates. Marty (along with his wife, Melanie) joined in the ongoing catechumenate sessions for a brief period but at the same time was meeting with his sponsor. Steve, a former minister, was given some materials to read regarding reconciliation and then met with the pastor, the catechumenate director and his sponsor for discussion and sharing concerning this sacrament. David (along with his wife) was guided through his preparation by a married couple who worked in Marriage Encounter. Together, as a way of discovering how God was present in David's life, they explored the church's understanding of matrimony and how this understanding is reflected within their own marriage. In each of these cases, the sacrament of penance was celebrated using the rite for individual penitents. This celebration was a part of their spiritual preparation for reception into the church, which for each of them occurred at different times of the year.

St. Margaret Mary church in Algonquin, Illinois, made particular arrangements in two cases. In the first situation, Louie, who had been attending Mass with his wife for 12 years, came forward desiring to become Catholic. He was prompted by the good things he was hearing about the catechumenate ministry in the parish. In the course of the initial interviews, the director informed Louie that he probably wouldn't need to participate in the full catechumenate. Louie insisted, however, that he wished to do so because the presence of the catechumenate in the parish was the very thing that stirred up his desire. He was introduced to the catechumenate group in a very simple manner, and he joined them for several months during their weekly catechetical sessions (but not the Sunday dismissal).

The second situation occurred the same year. Betty, who had been participating in Sunday Mass for 27 years, recognized the rightness for her of being received into the church. Through the initial interviews, the catechumenate director and pastor discerned that Betty was well catechized. Following the recommendation of the parish leaders and the willingness of the members of the RENEW group of which Betty had been a part, she entered into a period of preparation. The RENEW group gathered weekly for six weeks to participate in deep faith-sharing, reflection and retreat focused around Betty's journey toward reception. Just prior to the feast of Christ the King, both Louie and Betty, joined by their respective support communities, sponsors and Catholic family members, gathered for a communal penance celebration with individual confession and absolution. Then, on the feast of Christ the King, they were received into the full communion of the Catholic church.

St. Louise church in Bellevue, Washington, took an interesting approach to their outreach. The catechumenate director ran the following announcement in the parish bulletin several Sundays in a row early in the new year (January and February).

> BECOMING CATHOLIC Are you the spouse of a Catholic, who has perhaps been attending Mass here for many years, feeling yourself Catholic in many ways but just never having formalized it? Are you interested in completing that relationship by formally making a profession of faith, being confirmed and taking an active part at the eucharistic table? The year-long catechumenate process may not be needed for everyone. Please call [name and telephone number] if you might be interested in discussing further how you might complete your initiation into the Catholic faith.

After the first time this announcement ran in the bulletin, two men called the catechumenate director. Bill said to her, "I read the note you wrote to me in this week's bulletin." The other man, Mike, said that his wife shared the announcement with him and indicated that she felt it was addressed to him. Both men entered into a discernment process that verified not only their long-time desire but also their readiness to be received into the church.

They officially began their preparation at the parish's celebration of the combined form of the rite of sending (#530–546, U.S.

only). After testimonies and affirmations for the catechumens and candidates were gathered from the assembly, these new journeyers were presented. Brief comments regarding their background in the parish were made, including the fact that many of those who knew either one or both of these men probably thought they were already full members of the Catholic church. Testimony to their readiness and desire was given, and the assembly ratified the movement of God within the lives of these two men.

Throughout Lent, they gathered with the catechumenate group for their spiritual preparation and participated in the reflection sessions prior to the scrutinies. During the liturgies, however, they did not take on the role of recipients of the assembly's prayer but instead took their place as active members within the assembly praying over the catechumens. They were not dismissed with the catechumens and candidates but remained for the liturgy of the eucharist. Afterward, along with their sponsors, they joined those who had been dismissed, the catechumens' godparents, the candidates' sponsors and other team members for an extended time of reflection and prayer that built upon the liturgy just celebrated. Bill and Mike celebrated the sacrament of reconciliation in the same way the other baptized candidates of the parish did (see chapter 7).

St. Augustine parish had a similar experience. One year, Mary came forward on her own initiative just prior to the beginning of Lent. It was decided that in addition to meeting periodically with a parish catechist and her sponsor, Mary would join with the catechumenate group in their spiritual preparation during Lent, continue to meet with them through mystagogy and culminate her initiation by celebrating reception sometime during the Easter season.

Although Holy Cross parish in Regina, Saskatchewan, included catechized Christians in the parish catechumenate, they always made a conscious effort not only to respect but also to recognize their previous catechetical formation. As various aspects of the church's teachings and practices were discussed, the team invited the catechized Christians to share how a particular aspect of Catholicism was similar to or different from the approach of the community in which they had been formed. In those areas where there were differences, an explanation was given as to how or why the Catholic church approaches the issue differently. (St. Louise parish also did this with their catechized Christian candidates.)

REFLECTION ON THE PASTORAL RESPONSES

Like anyone who comes forward with an interest in the Catholic church, the baptized Christian deserves our attention to both his or her past (what the journey of faith has been thus far) as well as present (what God is prompting now). During this initial phase, it is important for the initiation team members to keep in mind Most Holy Trinity's guidelines, especially numbers one through four (see the section titled "Summary of the Process" in chapter 1, page 21), and Rita Ferrone's three movements (see the section "Three Movements" in chapter 2, pages 40 – 42).

During the first few times together, team members need to be open to the individual's story. Only after gaining a sense of the person should the parish's initiation process be brought into the dialogue. What of it is needed? What is not needed? What needs to be offered? As a part of the storytelling, listeners need to be attuned to identifying what particular gifts in Catholicism are attracting this candidate to our community (Ferrone's first movement).

Having heard the pertinent stories, the initiation team members and the baptized person can discern together what is needed to serve this person's growth in faith within our community. A framework for this discernment is provided by the four dimensions of catechesis (word, worship, service and community). The first step is to identify where the individual is within the spectrum of each of these dimensions. I find that working within the framework of a continuum[1] for each is helpful:

	Word	
literalist understanding	<———>	understanding its meaning

	Worship	
privatistic prayer	<———>	public worship

	Service	
concern for one's own salvation	<———>	witnessing for the salvation of the world

	Community	
rugged individualism	<———>	communal interdependence

As a part of identifying where a person is on each continuum, we ask, What gifts does this candidate bring from his or her community of origin (Ferrone's second movement)? The next step, then, is identifying what is needed to initiate or foster continued growth, helping each person to respond to God's call to ongoing conversion, to deeper holiness (Ferrone's third movement).

Having set up this tool for discernment, I want one thing to be clear: Although the ultimate goal of conversion is a life of faith that is grounded in the meaning of the scriptures, supported by public worship, made manifest in a life of service and carried out in the midst of a community, readiness for reception is not determined by whether or not one has reached the ultimate goal but by whether or not one is moving forward in the conversion process. The four-continua framework is an aid for discerning where a person is on his or her faith journey and what is needed to help that person be able to respond to the grace of God, which is drawing her or him further away from sin and deeper into the mystery of God's love. This discernment will help determine what is needed for ongoing pastoral formation and spiritual preparation prior to reception into the church.

In the pastoral responses concerning baptized, catechized adults, the only parish that included some ritual celebration of transition (using the rite of sending candidates for recognition and its corollary rite of calling candidates to continuing conversion) was St. Louise. As noted, these celebrations were not developed specifically for the baptized, catechized candidates, but in this case adaptation was made to include an introduction of the new journeyers. The other parishes recognized the transition that the catechized people were making, although they generally did not do so in ritual form or with a Sunday assembly.

After their needs are identified, some candidates enter into a period of further catechetical formation and others enter directly into a time of spiritual preparation for the celebration of reception. In either case, there is a transition in the journey to the eucharistic table. Although the order of initiation doesn't presume or require the celebration of any rituals other than the sacrament of penance when preparing for the rite of reception into the full communion of the Catholic church (as outlined in part II, chapter 5, of the *Rite of Christian Initiation of Adults*), it is good pastoral practice to ritualize the transition into the next stage. When the next stage is one of further formation, a simplified celebration of the rite of welcome may be appropriate. When the candidate is to move directly into a period of spiritual formation (or has completed a period of pastoral formation), a simplified celebration of the Rite of Calling Candidates to Continuing Conversion may be in order. In both situations, it would be most appropriate to celebrate these transitional rites with the Sunday assembly with whom the rite of reception will eventually be celebrated. This provides an opportunity for drawing an assembly into the initiation process and also catechizes them about the process of reception into the church.

DISMISSING THE CANDIDATES

In the cases reported in the first half of this chapter, there are differences in the ways various parishes approach the issue of dismissing the baptized, catechized candidate. Chapter 6 addressed this issue in reference to baptized, uncatechized candidates, but it merits further consideration in regard to catechized candidates.

Baptized, catechized candidates are likely, in most cases, to have some relationship with the Sunday assembly. Some may even have come to our eucharistic assembly from another eucharistic community and thus bring a theology and practice of communion. If there is to be a period of pastoral formation for these candidates, it is likely to be brief. Thus it is probably not advisable to invite them to participate in the regular Sunday dismissal of the catechumens and uncatechized candidates. Introducing a new person into this sharing process will disrupt the interpersonal dynamics already established; the new dynamics that will then be established will be disrupted once again when the catechized candidate moves out of this formation into the final period of preparation. More will be lost than gained in such an arrangement.

During the final period of spiritual preparation, however, a dismissal experience developed for the catechized candidate(s) may be considered. This dismissal would be based on the church's ancient practice of the paschal fast, which we continue to keep even now during the Easter Triduum. The paschal fast is an anticipatory fast, not a penitential fast. In anticipation of all the sacraments to be celebrated with abundant symbols at the Easter Vigil, the church fasts from all sacraments on Good Friday and Holy Saturday. So, too, it may be appropriate for these candidates to enter a "paschal fast" as they anticipate their reception into the church even when it is occurring at a time other than the Easter Vigil. Their "paschal fast" would occur on the Sundays between the ritual celebration of their transition into this final period of preparation and their reception.

By keeping this fast—that is, by not participating in the eucharistic prayer of thanks and praise—the candidates' sense of anticipation will be heightened and the assembly's awareness of the pending reception will be increased, drawing them into this time of prayerful preparation. The celebration of reception will derive added meaning from the enhanced sense of what it means to become one with us at the eucharistic table. As with the uncatechized candidates, the opportunity to participate in this dismissal experience should be presented as an invitation, not as an expectation.

SPIRITUAL PREPARATION PRIOR TO RECEPTION

How long is the period of spiritual preparation? What happens during this final period?

For the catechized Christian, there is no prescribed length of time for this period. In the cases presented, those who approached this period as distinct from the formation time generally used a six-week time frame. My inclination is to consider a period of three to six weeks, depending on the individuals involved and what has preceded it. If a period of pastoral formation has been a part of the process, a shorter period would probably suffice. If the candidates are entering directly into this preparation period, a longer time frame may be needed. In either situation, the time set aside for this period must be such that it will allow the dynamics of the period to unfold.

What happens during this time is shaped by keeping the vision of initiation in focus (Most Holy Trinity's guideline #4; see chapter I). This final period of preparation in the initiation rite has a penitential character. Penitential services that prepare for and lead into a celebration of the sacrament of penance are appropriate. Using the baptismal promises as the basis for the reflections and penitential rites (as might be done with uncatechized candidates preparing for reception) would be appropriate, because their reception into the Catholic church is building on their baptism.

Most Holy Trinity's guideline #6 ("Some type of prayer or retreat needs to be planned") merits consideration. This is an excellent time to plan a weekend away for a retreat. On Sundays, special blessings can be prayed over these candidates (either at the time of dismissal or at the end of Mass if they are not dismissed). The prayers for strength in the Canadian text provide a good sample of such a blessing (#491 Can.).

CONCLUSION

When considering the reception of a baptized, catechized adult, initiation ministers often tend toward one of two formats: They revert to the former "convert instruction" approach, with a quasi-private celebration of reception, or they move hastily into the rite of reception into the full communion of the Catholic church. In both situations, the vision of the order of Christian initiation has been lost. It is true that "no greater burden than is necessary is required" (#473 U.S., 387 Can.), but that does not mean that attention should not be given to providing appropriate pastoral formation and spiritual preparation. *The Rite of Christian Initiation of Adults* does not give exact direction concerning these situations because it presumes that the vision presented in part I of its text is understood by the initiation ministers and will be adapted to their pastoral situation and the people who come seeking reception. This echoes my point in chapter 5 (page 75) that even if a parish never initiates an unbaptized adult, it needs to be familiar with the normative elements for initiation as outlined in part one.

ENDNOTES

1. John Butler of St. Augustine Parish in Washington, D.C., provided the basic idea for this four-continua framework. His ideas were written up by James Dunning in his article "What Is a Catechized Adult?" *Forum Newsletter* 9, no. 2 (Summer 1992), 1.

CHAPTER NINE

Celebrating a New Union

RONALD A. OAKHAM

*N., of your own free will you have asked to be received into the full commu-
nion of the Catholic Church. You have made your decision after careful thought
under the guidance of the Holy Spirit. I now invite you to come forward with
your sponsor and in the presence of this community to profess the Catholic
faith. In this faith you will be one with us for the first time at the eucharistic
table of the Lord Jesus, the sign of the Church's unity.* (#490 U.S., 403 Can.)

When the pastoral formation of baptized candidates coincides with the pastoral formation of catechumens, reception into the full communion of the Catholic church generally occurs during the liturgy of baptism at the Easter Vigil using a combined form of these initiation rites (#562–594 U.S., 418–451 Can.). *The Rite of Christian Initiation of Adults,* however, not only allows for but in fact indicates that it prefers receiving baptized Christians at times other than the Easter Vigil. In my interviews with parish intiation ministers, I wanted to find out whether or not any parishes are receiving people at other times, and if so, when and how. As noted in the preceding chapters, I found some parishes that are doing so—but they are few in number.

PASTORAL RESPONSES

In the last chapter, the section on pastoral responses included the story of Mary, a baptized, catechized Christian who came to St. Augustine parish in Washington, D.C., just before Lent with a desire to become a Catholic. This section will begin with the continuation of her story.

As part of the decision regarding Mary's preparation for reception, the catechumenate director realized that the archdiocese of Washington, D.C., was going to be celebrating confirmation for adults at the cathedral during the Easter season. The director thought that this timing might work well with Mary's preparation. In addition, it would be an appropriate occasion to celebrate her reception. When approached about the possibility of including her reception in the confirmation celebration, the diocesan leadership was willing to do so. As anticipated, Mary was ready, and she was received into the church during this diocesan event.

Mary, Mother of the Church parish in St. Louis, Missouri, has celebrated reception, mostly with catechized candidates, at different times during the liturgical year, depending on the readiness of any candidates. One year they celebrated it on the feast of the Baptism of the Lord, highlighting ongoing growth in faith and fidelity to an earlier baptismal commitment. Another year, Trinity Sunday was the setting. Emphasis was given to the Creed as our statement of belief in a triune God. All Saints Day was chosen another time. On this occasion, the homily focused on the first reading, which spoke about those who were wearing white robes.

St. Louise parish in Bellevue, Washington, also has celebrated reception at other times, but usually for baptized candidates who, though ready at the time, were not able to be received at the Easter Vigil due to pending marriage cases. If the annulments were granted during the Easter Season, they would celebrate reception on Pentecost. If they were granted during the summer or fall, the candidates were received on the Feast of Christ the King.

The practice at St. Marcelline parish in Schaumburg, Illinois, has undergone several stages of development. Initially, baptized Christians were received into the church on one of the Sundays of Easter. But after some critical review, the initiation team decided that if the candidates were ready at Easter, their reception would be celebrated at the Easter Vigil. In addition, with the development of an ongoing process, they began to schedule a second celebration of reception each year. At first, the second celebration of reception took place during the parish's Thanksgiving Day Mass. But after more critical review, the team decided that a solemnity of the church was a more appropriate time. So they moved the celebration to the feast of Christ the King.

St. Philip parish in Bakersfield, California, also celebrates reception on the feast of Christ the King. In addition, they celebrate the rite on Pentecost and during February, prior to the beginning of Lent, if other candidates are ready at those times. If reception is celebrated in February, the Sunday with the most appropriate readings is selected.

In all of these parishes, except St. Augustine, the rite is celebrated with a Sunday assembly. The candidates and their sponsors generally take part in the opening procession. Whether they sit together in a reserved area or are scattered throughout the assembly varies from parish to parish. The option for the rite of sprinkling during the introductory rites of the Mass is usually chosen. During the rite of reception, the candidates may be called forward to gather in the altar area and face the assembly, or they may take their places in the aisles throughout the assembly. At the time of confirmation, the newly received gather together in the altar area (if they have not done so already). Some parishes include the newly received in the presentation of the gifts, some do not. What also varies is whether communion is distributed to them as a group prior to the assembly's communion sharing (in these cases they usually are invited to gather as a group near the altar), or they are interspersed among the assembly.

In two cases that I learned of, reception was celebrated in a quasi-private fashion with only a small gathering of friends. In one case the celebration took place outside Sunday Mass; in the other, it was celebrated within a Mass. (These stories were related to me by Rita Ferrone, who knew of these situations through her role as director for the catechumenate for the archdiocese of New York.)

In the first situation, after considerable discernment the pastor of a Lutheran parish near the Catholic parish where this took place had made the decision to enter into the full communion of the Catholic church. Several factors guided the parish leadership in their decision to celebrate his reception with a small assembly outside of Mass. The date selected for the celebration was the feast of the Assumption. Because of the holy day schedule, each of the priests of the parish would be presiding at a number of Masses. To add another Mass to the day did not seem prudent. In addition, they decided not to include the reception in one of the Assumption Masses to be ecumenically sensitive; they feared that doing so could be misconstrued as triumphalism, which is to "be carefully avoided" (#475.2 U.S., 389.2 Can.). In addition, many of the people who were to gather in support of the person were members of the Lutheran church and thus would not be able to participate fully in the eucharist in the Catholic church. To have celebrated the eucharist would have been a contradictory sign, heightening the fragmentation within the Christian community while celebrating a new union.

The second situation also was a decision based on pastoral sensitivity. In this case, the young woman to be received was experiencing considerable opposition from her parents regarding her decision. So great was their opposition that they threatened to interrupt the rite in protest. In order to avoid this confrontation within a liturgical setting, the pastoral team made the decision to celebrate her reception during a special Mass to which a small number of supporters from the parish would be invited.

REFLECTIONS ON PASTORAL RESPONSES

WITHIN MASS OR OUTSIDE MASS

Although the majority of responses indicated that reception is celebrated within the context of a Mass, the approach taken in the case

of the Lutheran priest was not aberrant. The order of initiation offers
the option of celebrating reception outside of Mass, although this is
not preferred, nor is it presented with the expectation that it will be
the form normally used (see the section "The Rite of Reception" in
chapter 2 of this book).

> The rite should appear clearly as a celebration of the
> church and have as its high point eucharistic communion.
> For this reason the rite should normally take place within
> Mass. (#475.1 U.S., 389.1 Can.)
>
> If the rite of reception is celebrated outside Mass, the
> Mass in which for the first time the newly received will
> take part with the Catholic community should be cele-
> brated as soon as possible, in order to make clear the con-
> nection between the reception and eucharistic communion.
> (#476 U.S., 390 Can.)

Even without these explicit statements in the introduction to the rite,
the proper setting can be determined by looking at the ritual itself. It
is a rite of reception *into the full communion* of the Catholic church.
Although key elements of the rite are the candidate's profession of faith
in the Catholic church, the church's welcome and the sacrament of confirmation, becoming one in the eucharistic sharing for the first time is
the culminating symbol. The goal is to become one with us at the
eucharistic table. Therefore, the primary setting for reception is within
a eucharistic celebration. Any other context is clearly an exception.

At the Easter Vigil, on a Solemnity or Sunday, or at Another Time

The majority of receptions take place during the Easter Vigil because,
in most cases, the candidates have been blended into the parish catechumenate. In addition, many catechumenate leaders consider the Easter
Vigil to be the only time adult initiation is permitted (a misreading
of the ritual text). But questions have been raised regarding whether
or not the Easter Vigil is the appropriate setting. In St. Marcelline's

story, we read that they used to initiate the catechumens at the Easter Vigil but received the candidates on another Sunday during Eastertime. Their original decision was prompted by their reading of the order, which for many presents a dilemma. The order seeks, however, to establish a priority among the many possibilities rather than to present a dilemma.

The introduction for the ritual of reception (#473–486 U.S., 376–386 Can.) gives no indication of the occasion on which the rite is to be celebrated. However, the opening rubric makes it clear that the intention is not to have it during the Easter Vigil:

> If the rite of reception into full communion takes place
> on a solemnity or on a Sunday, the Mass of the day should
> be celebrated; on other days it is permissible to celebrate
> the Mass "For the Unity of Christians" from the Masses
> for Various Needs. (#487 U.S., 400 Can.)

Yet the introduction at the beginning of part II, section 4, "Preparation of Uncatechized Adults for Confirmation and Eucharist," presents another view: "The high point of [the baptized Christians'] entire formation will normally be the Easter Vigil" (#409 U.S., 385 Can.). In addition, the order includes a combined rite for the Easter Vigil (#566–594 U.S., 422–451 Can.).

The U.S. edition seems to clarify this seeming contradiction in its National Statutes, which state, "The reception of candidates into the full communion of the Catholic church should ordinarily take place at the Sunday Eucharist of the parish community" (National Statutes, #32, U.S. only), and, "It is preferable that reception into full communion not take place at the Easter Vigil" (National Statutes, #33, U.S. only). But it then contributes to the confusion when, in the very next statute, it states:

> Nevertheless if there are both catechumens to be baptized
> and baptized Christians to be received into full commu-
> nion at the Vigil, for pastoral reasons in view of the Vigil's
> being the principal annual celebration of the church, the
> combined rite is to be followed. (#34 U.S. only)

In addressing this seeming dilemma, it is important to note that some of the confusion is rooted in the history of the development of this rite. The provisional text of the *Rite of Christian Initiation of Adults*, published in English in 1974, did not include the rite of reception into the full communion of the Catholic church. This rite was published separately at a later date. The provisional text did include, however, a chapter titled "Preparing Uncatechized Adults for Confirmation and the Eucharist,"[1] but it was unclear whether this chapter was designed for baptized, uncatechized Christians preparing for reception or for Catholics who, after having been baptized as infants, had no further catechetical formation and had not celebrated confirmation and/or first communion. Many presumed the latter because it made no reference to celebrating the rite of reception at the end of pastoral formation.

During the years in which the implementation of the catechumenate was guided by the provisional text, catechumenate ministers became aware that many baptized Christians seeking to be received into the full communion of the Catholic church were indeed uncatechized and needed a catechumenate-like formation (like that recommended in chapter 4 of the 1974 provisional text). Although no clear direction was given in the provisional text, catechumenate directors implemented their own adaptations and began to include baptized Christians in the parish's catechumenate and to receive them into the church at the Easter Vigil in a combined rite.

In 1985, the International Commission on English in the Liturgy (ICEL) revised the *Rite of Christian Initiation of Adults.* This revision was then sent to the bishops of English-speaking countries to adopt as their own or to use as the basis for further pastoral revisions for use in their own countries. The revision by ICEL only partially addressed the developing confusion: It rearranged the structure of the provisional text, incorporating the rite of reception into the body of the order (part II, section 5), and it added a combined rite for the Easter Vigil in an appendix. It did not, however, clarify to whom part II, section 4 (the preparation of uncatechized adults) was referring.

The subcommittee of the United States Bishops' Committee on the Liturgy that worked to develop the U.S. edition of the order sought to ease the confusion by editing the opening paragraph of part II, section 4, to read:

> The following pastoral guidelines concern adults who were baptized as infants *either as Roman Catholics or as members of another Christian community* but did not receive further catechetical formation. (#400 U.S. only, italics identify addition)

This editorial addition in the U.S. text helps clarify that the order is concerned with several different pastoral situations involving baptized adults: the reception of baptized, *catechized* Christians; the reception of baptized, *uncatechized* Christians; and the completion of the initiation of baptized, *uncatechized Catholics.*

The rite of reception is used for baptized Christians from other denominations, but the context within which it is celebrated may vary according to the situations of the persons with whom it is celebrated: With the catechized Christian, it is ordinarily celebrated on a solemnity or on a Sunday; with the uncatechized Christian it may be celebrated on a solemnity or a Sunday, or for pastoral reasons, at the Easter Vigil, being sure to avoid "anything that would equate them with catechumens" (#565 U.S., 421 Can.). The order also allows, for good pastoral reasons, the completion of the initiation of uncatechized Catholics at the Easter Vigil with the celebration of confirmation[2] and eucharist (#409 U.S., 385 Can.).

The question is not whether baptized adults may be received or may complete their initiation at the Easter Vigil. The question we must deal with is whether or not it is the most appropriate context.

Including candidates may, in some cases, cause the number of people being initiated and received at the Easter Vigil to be quite large. In such cases, some ministers might be tempted to simplify or downplay the initiation rites for the sake of efficiency. But this would diminish the power of the rituals to celebrate and to catechize about new life. Rather than compromise the rites, the better pastoral approach would be to use the options available for the best celebrations in all situations. This is what St. Philip and St. Marcelline parishes have done. They both have a large number of catechumens being baptized each Easter Vigil, so they have removed the receptions from that setting and celebrate them fully at other times.

It could also be that some candidates, though ready, cannot be received at the Easter Vigil due to pending marriage cases, or that some candidates may not be ready personally. When their marriage cases are resolved or when the candidates reach personal readiness, they do not have to wait until the next Easter Vigil but can be received on an appropriate solemnity or Sunday.

Concerning baptized, catechized Christians, the order presumes that they are not a part of the parish's catechumenate but are provided with a simpler preparation developed in response to their needs. At the appropriate time, their reception would ordinarily take place on a solemnity or a Sunday, not at the Easter Vigil. In addition to catechized Christians, some previously uncatechized Christians who are now completing their pastoral formation may also participate in this celebration.

Although it does so subtly, the ritual text includes an order of preference for when reception occurs (see #487 U.S., 400 Can.); celebrating reception on a day other than the Easter Vigil, a Sunday or a solemnity is a last choice. More critical than when reception will be celebrated is the matter of whether it will be experienced as a "celebration of the church" (#475.1 U.S., 389.1 Can.). Will the church be present in the fullest form available—in the full, conscious and active participation of a representative body of the parish community—or will reception be experienced as a quasi-private celebration of the catechumenal community (a subgroup of the parish and the church at large) along with some personal relatives and friends? Ecclesial sensitivity needs to be weighed with ecumenical and pastoral sensitivities.

How Often and When to Celebrate

Once a parish understands that it has options in addition to the Easter Vigil, it must decide how often and when reception should be celebrated. The text is not specific about how often, however; the recommendation it makes concerning the rite of acceptance into the order of catechumens—that it may be celebrated on "two dates in the year, or three if necessary" (#18.3)—provides a good guideline.

In choosing these two (or, if necessary, three) dates, it is important to remember the norm for selecting the time of initiation: individual and communal readiness. Although we are considering the readiness of one or more individuals at any given time, we also are concerned with celebrating a rite that belongs to the church itself. The decision of when to celebrate the rite must include consideration not only of when the individuals being received are ready but also of when the community (the church) is ready to enter fully into this action. The best guide for determining this readiness is the liturgical calendar.

Relying on the liturgical calendar means taking into consideration the ebb and flow of the liturgical year as a whole as well as any given solemnity or Sunday within the year. In the parishes discussed earlier in this chapter, the liturgical calendar was taken into consideration: Choosing the Feast of Christ the King, the final Sunday of the liturgical year, leads naturally into a new cycle; All Saints Day celebrates the full scope of the church; or a particular Sunday in late January or early February is chosen because the readings provide a natural context for reception. A question to consider when trying to decide when to celebrate reception is, Will the inclusion of the rite of reception, with the presence of the candidates and the action of the assembly, enflesh what is being proclaimed in the word, or will it be experienced as an unrelated appendage to this particular gathering?

Mary, Mother of the Church parish's choice of various solemnities demonstrates the sense of congruence between the liturgy of the day and the ritual celebration. For example, when they celebrate reception on the feast of the Baptism of the Lord, they highlight ongoing growth in faith and fidelity to an earlier baptismal commitment to which this feast annually calls all of us. In that particular year, the presence of some adults who had been doing just that helped enflesh the message of the readings.

An example of incongruence would be to choose (because it is convenient) the Thirty-first Sunday in Ordinary Time during Year A. The first reading has God lashing out against the priests of the community who have broken faith, "profaning the covenant of our ancestors" (Deuteronomy 6: 2–6). The gospel admonishes the Israelites not to be guided by what the scribes and Pharisees do and say, because "they do not practice what they preach" (Matthew 23:1–12). Although these readings do present good challenges for each and every age, they do not create an appropriate setting within which to celebrate reception.

RECEIVING COMMUNION

The final item I want to reflect on in this chapter is the manner in which the newly received share in the eating and drinking at the eucharist. The pastoral responses presented in this chapter reflect two basic patterns: receiving communion as a particular group prior to the assembly's communion sharing, and being interspersed among the assembly.

In the early years of implementation, the team with which I was ministering decided to have the neophytes receive as a group prior to the assembly's communion. Upon reflection, though, the catechumenate team was not pleased with what it was hearing. Most often it reflected a privatistic sense of communion. The neophytes spoke only of their joy at being able to receive the Lord in his body and blood; something was missing. We began to recognize that our discomfort with the way we arranged the reception of the eucharist by the newly received resulted from the clash of the various experiences we had allowed to influence our decisions: the practices of children's first communion, social etiquette and the symbolic expression of what it means to be church.

At first communion celebrations in most places, it is the custom to give communion to the children as a group prior to giving it to the assembly. We began to wonder whether this pattern was the product of a particular situation within our church. For a long period of our church's history, first communions occurred within an assembly that, for the most part, didn't go to communion. Would a different pattern have emerged if the assembly were receiving communion?

Second, social etiquette prompts us to allow guests of honor to go first. But does arranging for a separate sharing of the eucharist symbolize what we are celebrating—their oneness with us at the table of the Lord? As we analyzed this practice, separating the newly received from the assembly at this point was proclaiming less a new community union and more a newly gained personal right—to receive communion.

But we believed that the rite seeks to proclaim a new relationship, a sharing of a new union with these new members, a deeper oneness in the Lord begun in our common baptism. Because of this, we join together in sharing the one bread and the one cup. This symbolic expression of what it means to be church contrasted with what we were hearing in the mystagogical reflections.

Thus, we changed our practice. The newly received are interspersed among the assembly as they all share in the eucharist. This is not to say that appropriate recognition of this new step is not made; prior to distributing communion, the newly received are addressed following the suggestion made in the rubrics:

> Before saying "This is the Lamb of God," the celebrant
> may briefly remind the neophytes of the preeminence of
> the eucharist, which is the climax of their initiation and
> the center of the whole Christian life. (#243, repeated in
> 594 U.S.; 233, repeated in 451 Can.)

My comments to those about to receive communion with us for the first time usually begin by referring to the line in one of the dismissal formularies, "We look forward to the day when you will share fully in the Lord's table" (#67B, U.S. only). After indicating that this is that longed-for day, I tell about the joy it brings to our community and then invite them to share with us our sacred meal. Their sponsors accompany them, modeling for them how to take communion and staying with them as they partake of the eucharist.

Their reflections after we made this change were filled with images of becoming fully one with the Lord and with the community.

When we heard this, we knew that symbolic actions rightfully had taken precedence over a long-standing custom and social etiquette.

CONCLUSION

With the renewal of the catechumenate and the restoration of adult baptism into the mainstream of parish life, initiation ministers often get swept up with the awesome meaning that flows from immersion baptisms. Unfortunately (as was discussed in chapter 6), this has a tendency to shorten the horizons toward which we journey with both unbaptized and baptized alike. The church's revised rites of initiation challenge us to journey not just to the font of baptism but through it to a table of unity. When we allow the rite of reception into the full communion of the Catholic church to take its rightful place within our initiation rites, and when we begin to breathe the same amount of life into it that we have been doing with the catechumenal rites, I believe our sights will be drawn outward to the furthest horizon of our faith—to where all God's people will be celebrating a new union: that new world where the fullness of Christ's peace will be revealed, where people of every race, language, and way of life will be gathered to share in the one eternal banquet with Jesus Christ the Lord (see Eucharistic Prayer for Reconciliation II).

ENDNOTES

1. International Committee on English in the Liturgy, *Rite of Christian Initiation of Adults* (Washington DC: National Conference of Catholic Bishops, 1974), 99–100.

2. In situations where an unbaptized adult is being initiated or a baptized Christian is being received, the priest who has the faculties to baptize and receive them, by virtue of liturgical law, has the faculty to confirm (see *Code of Canon Law*, #883). In the case of baptized Catholics completing their initiation, however, the faculty to confirm is not to be presumed. In most cases, a request for delegation of the faculty must be made to the bishop or other assigned authority in the diocese, if

some diocesan regulation regarding this issue has not already been put into place. To determine when delegation is needed, see the comments regarding canon 883 in James Coriden et. al. *The Code of Canon Law: A Text and Commentary* (Mahwah: Paulist Press, 1985), 635–637. The pertinent paragraph of this comment is included in the National Statutes of the U.S. edition, #28.

CHAPTER TEN

Unfolding the Mysteries

RONALD A. OAKHAM

These adults will complete their Christian formation and become fully inte-
grated into the community by going through the period of postbaptismal catech-
esis or mystagogy. (#410 U.S., 386 Can.)

The period of mystagogy, during which mysteries
—the sacraments—are unfolded, has proven to
be one of the more elusive areas of implementation
in the catechumenate. Knowing this, I expected to
find that mystagogy is even less successfully implemented with the reception of baptized Christians.
My expectations were met. In almost all the parishes I interviewed,
except for those described in this chapter, little is happening.

PASTORAL RESPONSES

Mary, Mother of the Church parish meets with the newly received
for about four weeks after reception. During these sessions they
explore the sacraments of confirmation and eucharist. They don't
meet again after this.

St. Marcelline also meets for four weeks after the celebration of
reception. Like Mary, Mother of the Church parish, they use this
time to unfold the experience of the sacraments of confirmation and

eucharist. Following these weeks, they continue to gather monthly. At the end of the following Easter season, the group that has been meeting monthly welcomes the neophytes into the ongoing, monthly group after the neophytes have finished their own weekly mystagogical meetings.

St. Philip parish doesn't gather with the newly received the week immediately after the celebration but begins a series of weekly meetings the following week. This first meeting focuses on the reception celebration in general, allowing for a sharing about the experience. The catechists for these sessions listen closely, particularly for what is being said about the sacraments which the newly received are now celebrating. The newly received continue to meet with the catechists for several weeks, first exploring penance, confirmation and eucharist from their new perspective, then exploring the other sacraments.

In time, the meetings move to monthly gatherings, with members of the group taking responsibility for the sessions. They organize the meetings, and they pursue the others if they miss a session. Topics for study are chosen by the group, with members volunteering to be responsible for upcoming sessions. Members work with a catechist on the parish initiation team to gather materials and prepare. As at St. Marcelline, this group takes the lead in welcoming the next group of neophytes into the ongoing mystagogy.

INTERVIEWS WITH SOME NEWLY RECEIVED CATHOLICS

I met one evening with several people who had been received into the full communion of the Catholic church through the process established at St. Philip. Having heard the parish's story from the catechumenate director, I wanted to hear what those who had been through the parish's adapted process had to say about their experience. The individuals with whom I spoke represented several different groups, so their experiences varied as the parish process matured.

All were in agreement that although there wasn't an explicit effort within the process to help them develop a respect for their baptism, their respect and reverence for it did grow because the formation process was, as one person indicated, so imbued with a baptismal spirituality. A couple of participants expressed a desire that more prominence would have been given to the memory of their baptism. One specifically suggested that people might gather their stories about it and then share those stories. Another recommended that candidates should be encouraged to communicate with their godparents. (Some of the ideas in chapter 6 were influenced by this conversation.)

There was real evidence of continued development within the pastoral formation being offered. Some who had been through the process in the earlier years of its inception felt it was mostly Bible study. They wanted more time spent on Catholic teaching. Those who came through the process later felt that they had come to understand how the Catholic church had developed its teachings and practices in response to the message of the scriptures.

The rituals that marked the various steps along the way were appreciated by everyone. Memories of both the rite of welcome and the rite of reception still evoked a sense of awe and wonder in the group. As they talked about these rites, I could hear in their voices and see in their faces a great reverence for what they had experienced. The rite of welcome had brought the decision to deepen their faith life in the context of the Catholic community into clearer focus and had provided them an opportunity to commit to a plan of action. When they spoke about the rite of reception, I found it interesting that almost all of the conversation focused on sharing in the eucharist.

The rite of calling to continuing conversion and the sacrament of penance had mixed responses. Those who had celebrated the call to continuing conversion after the parish had begun to include the presentation of their baptismal certificates in the rite were better able to recall and speak about the rite than those who had celebrated it earlier. The responses to penance seemed to depend more on the individual's disposition about this particular sacrament than on the way it was celebrated.

When I inquired about not being received during the Easter Vigil but at another time, several said that they had had some initial resentment about the parish's policy, because the Easter Vigil was always being presented as the "big" event. Once they entered into the process, however, the issue of when they would be received became less important. When they did celebrate reception, they felt that it was a major focus of the parish's gathering that day. In comparing their experience with the thought of being received at the Easter Vigil, several said they wouldn't have wanted to do it then because so much emphasis is given to the baptisms. Some others indicated that they had been at an Easter Vigil that included both baptisms and receptions and had felt that the baptized candidates seemed out of place; they were happy to have been a part of a celebration in which only reception into the church was being celebrated. I found it interesting that, even though their receptions did not take place during the Easter Vigil, they all spoke of the Vigil with high regard and expressed an understanding of it as a sacred time in the life of our church.

REFLECTIONS ON THE PASTORAL RESPONSES

At the conclusion of chapter 6, I suggested that when we think about the formation of the baptized Christian, we need to think mystagogically. If initiation ministers approach the pastoral formation of catechumens and candidates in this way, they will be setting a firm foundation for a fruitful period of mystagogy.[1] But what does thinking mystagogically mean?

Two resources have helped me to understand what is meant by thinking mystagogically: the mystagogical homilies of Cyril of Jerusalem (a Father of the church during the first half of the fourth century)[2] and the principles of adult learning developed by Leon McKensie and Malcolm Knowles.[3] Cyril's homilies demonstrate the dynamic of taking one's experience of the initiation rites and bringing it into dialogue with stories from the scriptures in order to interpret (i.e., theologize about) what has happened. McKensie's and Knowles's principles of adult learning present adults as active and involved learners who do not need all the answers given to them but who can, with appropriate and sufficient information, draw the necessary conclusions themselves.

Blending these two elements together can create a mystagogical approach appropriate for contemporary adult catechesis. If catechists focus on working with the candidates to relate their own life stories to the stories in sacred scripture and the church's tradition in order to draw out Catholic theology, rather than focusing on presenting disembodied theological treatises, then candidates will be formed in mystagogical thinking. As a result, when they experience something new, such as the initiation sacraments, they will naturally want to explore the new meanings the experience presents. From their experiences during formation, they will know that there is always some new understanding to be had rather than believing that they have learned all there is to know.

This is, in fact, what happened at St. Philip. The initiation team had been working very hard to reform their catechetical style from a child-centered approach to an adult-centered approach. They had noticed that the more they relied on adult learning principles as a guide for developing their catechetical sessions, the more success they had with the period of mystagogy.

One of the major challenges facing initiation teams is that of reshaping their catechetical style into a more adult-centered approach. If we try to pass along our faith in didactic, data-filled lectures, we leave adults out of the learning circle. We treat them as mere receptacles into which we put our treasures. This approach will not foster adults' desire for learning but will repel them. Thus, when they achieve that for which they have come (reception into the full communion of the Catholic church), they will stop participating in any sessions. If, however, adults are treated as colearners in the process rather than as mere receptacles, their desire to continue to learn will be fostered, and mystagogy—drawing meaning from relating their experiences with the sacred scriptures and traditions of the church—will become a way of life for them.

IN CONCLUSION

Writing this book has been a mystagogical experience for me. It is the result of my deliberations on the experiences I have had in implementing the order of Christian initiation of adults and on my study of related materials in theology, liturgy, education, sociology and psychology. My thoughts have been ripened in conversations with other pastoral ministers, some who share my conclusions and others who do not. But whether they share my conclusions or not, each has been important in helping me clarify my thoughts. I hope the ideas presented in this book help others reflect critically on their own efforts to implement and adapt the order of initiation for baptized Christians who will become one with us at the table of the Lord.

ENDNOTES

1. See my article "Sowing for a Good Harvest: Underpinnings for Mystagogy" in *Catechumenate: A Journal of Christian Initiation* vol. 12, no. 1 (January 1990), in which I wrote about elements within the full catechumenate that bear on the eventual success or failure of the period of mystagogy.

2. See the bibliography for some resources that focus on mystagogy. These particular resources contain selections of texts from the mystagogical homilies of the Fathers of the church.

3. See the bibliography for resources by these leaders in adult education.

BIBLIOGRAPHY

BAIMA, THOMAS. "Building on the Faith that Candidates Bring, Part I." *Catechumenate: A Journal of Christian Initiation* 15, no. 3 (May, 1993): 20–27.

——. "Building on the Faith that Candidates Bring, Part II." *Catechumenate: A Journal of Christian Initiation* 15, no. 5 (September 1993): 2–9.

Canadian Conference of Catholic Bishops. *Rite of Christian Initiation of Adults.* Ottawa, Ontario, Canada: Publications Service, 1987.

DUNNING, JAMES. "What Is a Catechized Adult?" *Forum Newsletter* (North American Forum on the Catechumenate), 9, no. 2 (Summer 1992): 1, 4, 6.

FERRONE, RITA. *On the Rite of Election,* Forum Essays 3, Chicago: Liturgy Training Publications, 1994.

FIELD, OSB, ANNE. *From Darkness to Light: What It Meant to Become a Christian in the Early Church.* Ann Arbor, MI: Servant Books, 1978.

KNOWLES, MALCOLM. *Modern Practice of Adult Education: Andragogy Versus Pedagogy.* New York: Association Press, 1970.

LOGUE, JUDY. "Exceptional Circumstances: Nancy's Journey." *Catechumenate: A Journal of Christian Initiation* 15, no. 1 (January 1993): 2–8.

LOPRESTI, JAMES. "Scrutinies or Confession?" *Catechumenate: A Journal of Christian Initiation* 9, no. 4 (March 1987): 15–19.

MCKENSIE, LEON. *Adult Religious Education: The 20th Century Challenge.* West Mystic, CT: Twenty-Third Publications, 1975.

MAZZA, ENRICO. *Mystagogy.* New York: Pueblo Publishing Co., 1989.

MORRIS, THOMAS. "Open the Rite Door: Exploring Part II of the *Rite of Christian Initiation of Adults.*" *Catechumenate: A Journal of Christian Initiation* 15, no. 3 (May 1993): 10–19.

——. "The Rite Time." *Catechumenate: A Journal of Christian Initiation* 13, no. 3 (May 1991): 21–25.

National Conference of Catholic Bishops. *Rite of Christian Initiation of Adults.* Chicago: Liturgy Training Publications, 1988.

——. *Rite of Penance.* New York: Catholic Book Publishing Co., 1975.

OAKHAM, RONALD. "An 'International Configuration' of Initiation Rites: A Look at the Combined Rites of Appendix I." *Catechumenate: A Journal of Christian Initiation* 15, no. 4 (July 1993): 11–20.

————. "Baptized Candidates and the Lenten Rites." *Catechumenate: A Journal of Christian Initiation* 12, no. 6 (November 1990): 18–25.

————. "The Extended Mystagogy: Indictment or Wisdom?" *Catechumenate: A Journal of Christian Initiation* 14, no. 3 (May 1992): 17–23.

————. "Sorting Fish: A Task at the Beginning." *Catechumenate: A Journal of Christian Initiation* 11, no. 3 (May 1989): 13–19.

————. "Sowing for a Good Harvest: Underpinnings for Mystagogy." *Catechumenate: A Journal of Christian Initiation* 12, no. 1 (January 1990): 22–27.

REISER, WILLIAM. *Renewing the Baptismal Promises.* New York: Pueblo Publishing Co., 1988.

RILEY, HUGH. *Christian Initiation.* Vol. 17 of *Studies in Christian Antiquity,* ed. Johannes Quasten. Washington, D.C.: The Catholic University of America Press; Consortium Press, 1974.

TURNER, PAUL. "Forlorn Yet Privileged." *Forum Newsletter* (North American Forum on the Catechumenate) 11, no. 1 (Winter 1994): 3–4, 10.

WAGNER, NICK. "Muddy Waters: Welcoming Baptized, Catechized Christians into Full Communion." *Catechumenate: A Journal of Christian Initiation* 14, no. 3 (May 1992): 24–29.

YARNOLD, SJ, EDWARD. *The Awe-Inspiring Rites of Initiation: The Origins of the rcia,* second edition. Collegeville: The Liturgical Press, 1994.

KATHY BROWN is a member of the faculty of the Kino Foundation, a center for the education and training of ministers in Phoenix, Arizona. She has served as a parish and diocesan minister in positions concerning Christian initiation, liturgy and social justice and has worked as director of institutes for the North American Forum on the Catechumenate, for which she still serves as a team member. Kathy holds a master's degree in theology from St. Paul's University, Ottawa, Canada.

JOSEPH FAVAZZA is assistant professor of theology at Rhodes College in Memphis, Tennessee, and a consultant and team member for ReMembering Church, an institute of the North American Forum on the Catechumenate that focuses on people who are engaged in a process of reconciliation. He is the author of *The Order of Penitents: Historical Roots and Pastoral Future* (Collegeville: The Liturgical Press, 1988). Joe earned a doctorate at the Catholic University of Louvain, Belgium.

RITA FERRONE is director of the office of the catechumenate for the diocese of Allentown, Pennsylvania, a position in which she also served for four years in the archdiocese of New York. Rita is a team member for institutes of the North American Forum on the Catechumenate and is the author of *On the Rite of Election*, Forum Essay 3 (Chicago: Liturgy Training Publications, 1994). She holds a master of divinity degree from Yale University.

MARK SEARLE was professor of theology at the University of Notre Dame in Notre Dame, Indiana. His writings include *Christening: The Making of Christians* and *Liturgy Made Simple*, both from The Liturgical Press, and *The Church Speaks about Sacraments with Children*, from Liturgy Training Publications. He earned a doctorate from the Liturgical Institute at the University of Trier. Mark Searle died in 1992.

RONALD A. OAKHAM, a priest of the Carmelite order, is regional provincial of the southwest region of the Chicago province of Carmelites. Ron has been a pastor and the diocesan director of the catechumenate for the archdiocese of Newark, New Jersey. He served for a time as director of institutes for the North American Forum on the Catechumenate, for which he still serves as a team member. Ron holds a master's degree in theology from Washington Theological Union in Washington, D.C.